About the Reviewer

Mike Driscoll has been programming in Python since 2006. He enjoys writing about Python on his blog at `http://www.blog.pythonlibrary.org/`. He co-authored the *Core Python Refcard* for DZone. Mike has also been a technical reviewer for *Python 3 Object Oriented Programming*, *Python 2.6 Graphics Cookbook*, *Tkinter GUI Application Development Hotshot*, and several others. He recently wrote the book *Python 101*, and is working on his next book.

> I would like to thank my beautiful wife, Evangeline, for always supporting me. I would also like to thank friends and family for all that they do to help me. And I would like to thank Jesus Christ for saving me.

www.PacktPub.com

eBooks, discount offers, and more

Did you know that Packt offers eBook versions of every book published, with PDF and ePub files available? You can upgrade to the eBook version at www.PacktPub.com and as a print book customer, you are entitled to a discount on the eBook copy. Get in touch with us at customercare@packtpub.com for more details.

At www.PacktPub.com, you can also read a collection of free technical articles, sign up for a range of free newsletters and receive exclusive discounts and offers on Packt books and eBooks.

https://www2.packtpub.com/books/subscription/packtlib

Do you need instant solutions to your IT questions? PacktLib is Packt's online digital book library. Here, you can search, access, and read Packt's entire library of books.

Why subscribe?

- Fully searchable across every book published by Packt
- Copy and paste, print, and bookmark content
- On demand and accessible via a web browser

Table of Contents

Preface

Modular programming is a way of organizing your program's source code. By organizing your code into modules (Python source files) and packages (collections of modules), and then importing those modules and packages into your program, you can keep your programs logically organized and keep potential problems to a minimum.

As your program grows and changes, you will often have to rewrite or expand certain parts of your code. Modular programming techniques help to manage these changes, minimizing side-effects, and keeping your code under control.

As you work with modular programming techniques, you will learn a number of common patterns for using modules and packages, including the divide and conquer approach to programming, the use of abstraction and encapsulation, and the idea of writing extensible modules.

Modular programming techniques are also a great way of sharing your code, either by making it available for other people to use or by reusing your code in another program. Using popular tools such as GitHub and the Python Package Index, you will learn how to publish your code, as well as use code written by other people.

Putting all these techniques together, you will learn how apply "modular thinking" to create better programs. You will see how modules can be used to deal with complexity and change in a large program and how modular programming really is the foundation of good programming technique.

By the end of the book, you will have an excellent understanding of how modules and packages work in Python and how to use them to create high-quality and robust software that can be shared with others.

What this book covers

Chapter 1, Introducing Modular Programming, looks at the ways you can use Python modules and packages to help organize your programs, why it is important to use modular techniques, and how modular programming helps you to deal with the ongoing process of programming.

Chapter 2, Writing Your First Modular Program, introduces the *divide and conquer* approach to programming and applies this technique to the process of building an inventory control system based on modular programming principles.

Chapter 3, Using Modules and Packages, covers the nuts and bolts of modular programming using Python, including nested packages, package and module initialization techniques, relative imports, choosing what gets imported, and how to deal with circular references.

Chapter 4, Using Modules for Real-World Programming, uses the implementation of a chart-generation library to show how modular techniques help to deal with changing requirements in the best possible way.

Chapter 5, Working with Module Patterns, looks at a number of standard patterns for working with modules and packages, including the divide and conquer technique, abstraction, encapsulation, wrappers, and how to write extensible modules using dynamic imports, plugins, and hooks.

Chapter 6, Creating Reusable Modules, shows how to design and create modules and packages that are intended to be shared with other people.

Chapter 7, Advanced Module Techniques, looks at some of the more distinctive aspects of modular programming in Python, including optional and local imports, tweaking the module search path, "gotchas" to be aware of, how to use modules and packages for rapid application development, working with package globals, package configuration, and package data files.

Chapter 8, Testing and Deploying Modules, examines the concept of unit testing, how to prepare your modules and packages for publication, how to upload and publish your work, and how to make use of modules and packages written by other people.

Chapter 9, Modular Programming as a Foundation for Good Programming Technique, shows how modular techniques help to deal with the ongoing process of programming by dealing with change and managing complexity, and how modular programming techniques help you to be a more effective programmer.

What you need for this book

All you need to follow through the examples in this book is a computer running any recent version of Python. While the examples all use Python 3, they can easily be adapted to work with Python 2 only a few changes.

Who this book is for

This book is aimed at the beginner to intermediate level Python programmer who wishes to use modular programming techniques to create high-quality and well organized programs. While the reader must know the basics of Python, no prior knowledge of modular programming is required.

Conventions

In this book, you will find a number of text styles that distinguish between different kinds of information. Here are some examples of these styles and an explanation of their meaning.

Code words in text, database table names, folder names, filenames, file extensions, pathnames, dummy URLs, user input, and Twitter handles are shown as follows: " This one-line program would be saved in a file on disk, typically named something like `hello.py` "

A block of code is set as follows:

```
def init():
    global _stats
    _stats = {}
```

When we wish to draw your attention to a particular part of a code block, the relevant lines or items are set in bold:

```
[default]
exten => s,1,Dial(Zap/1|30)
exten => s,2,Voicemail(u100)
exten => s,102,Voicemail(b100)
exten => i,1,Voicemail(s0)
```

Any command-line input or output is written as follows:

```
# cp /usr/src/asterisk-addons/configs/cdr_mysql.conf.sample
    /etc/asterisk/cdr_mysql.conf
```

New terms and **important words** are shown in bold. Words that you see on the screen, for example, in menus or dialog boxes, appear in the text like this: "Clicking the **Next** button moves you to the next screen."

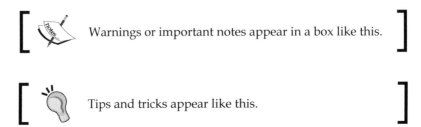

Warnings or important notes appear in a box like this.

Tips and tricks appear like this.

Reader feedback

Feedback from our readers is always welcome. Let us know what you think about this book—what you liked or disliked. Reader feedback is important for us as it helps us develop titles that you will really get the most out of.

To send us general feedback, simply e-mail feedback@packtpub.com, and mention the book's title in the subject of your message.

If there is a topic that you have expertise in and you are interested in either writing or contributing to a book, see our author guide at www.packtpub.com/authors.

Customer support

Now that you are the proud owner of a Packt book, we have a number of things to help you to get the most from your purchase.

Downloading the example code

You can download the example code files for this book from your account at http://www.packtpub.com. If you purchased this book elsewhere, you can visit http://www.packtpub.com/support and register to have the files e-mailed directly to you.

You can download the code files by following these steps:

1. Log in or register to our website using your e-mail address and password.
2. Hover the mouse pointer on the **SUPPORT** tab at the top.
3. Click on **Code Downloads & Errata**.

4. Enter the name of the book in the **Search** box.

5. Select the book for which you're looking to download the code files.

6. Choose from the drop-down menu where you purchased this book from.

7. Click on **Code Download**.

You can also download the code files by clicking on the **Code Files** button on the book's webpage at the Packt Publishing website. This page can be accessed by entering the book's name in the **Search** box. Please note that you need to be logged in to your Packt account.

Once the file is downloaded, please make sure that you unzip or extract the folder using the latest version of:

- WinRAR / 7-Zip for Windows
- Zipeg / iZip / UnRarX for Mac
- 7-Zip / PeaZip for Linux

The code bundle for the book is also hosted on GitHub at `https://github.com/PacktPublishing`/Modular-Programming-with-Python. We also have other code bundles from our rich catalog of books and videos available at `https://github.com/PacktPublishing/`. Check them out!

Errata

Although we have taken every care to ensure the accuracy of our content, mistakes do happen. If you find a mistake in one of our books—maybe a mistake in the text or the code—we would be grateful if you could report this to us. By doing so, you can save other readers from frustration and help us improve subsequent versions of this book. If you find any errata, please report them by visiting `http://www.packtpub.com/submit-errata`, selecting your book, clicking on the **Errata Submission Form** link, and entering the details of your errata. Once your errata are verified, your submission will be accepted and the errata will be uploaded to our website or added to any list of existing errata under the Errata section of that title.

To view the previously submitted errata, go to `https://www.packtpub.com/books/content/support` and enter the name of the book in the search field. The required information will appear under the **Errata** section.

Piracy

Piracy of copyrighted material on the Internet is an ongoing problem across all media. At Packt, we take the protection of our copyright and licenses very seriously. If you come across any illegal copies of our works in any form on the Internet, please provide us with the location address or website name immediately so that we can pursue a remedy.

Please contact us at copyright@packtpub.com with a link to the suspected pirated material.

We appreciate your help in protecting our authors and our ability to bring you valuable content.

Questions

If you have a problem with any aspect of this book, you can contact us at questions@packtpub.com, and we will do our best to address the problem.

1
Introducing Modular Programming

Modular programming is an essential tool for the modern developer. Gone are the days when you could just throw something together and hope that it works. To build robust systems that last, you need to understand how to organize your programs so that they can grow and evolve over time. *Spaghetti coding* is not an option. Modular programming techniques, and in particular the use of Python modules and packages, will give you the tools you need to succeed as a professional in the fast changing programming landscape.

In this chapter, we will:

- Look at the fundamental aspects of modular programming
- See how Python modules and packages can be used to organize your code
- Discover what happens when modular programming techniques are not used
- Learn how modular programming helps you stay on top of the development process
- Take a look at the Python standard library as an example of modular programming
- Create a simple program, built using modular techniques, to see how it works in practice

Let's get started by learning about modules and how they work.

Introducing Python modules

For most beginner programmers, their first Python program is some version of the famous *Hello World* program. This program would look something like this:

```
print("Hello World!")
```

This one-line program would be saved in a file on disk, typically named something like `hello.py`, and it would be executed by typing the following command into a terminal or command-line window:

python hello.py

The Python interpreter would then dutifully print out the message you have asked it to:

Hello World!

This `hello.py` file is called a **Python source file**. When you are first starting out, putting all your program code into a single source file is a great way of organizing your program. You can define functions and classes, and put instructions at the bottom which start your program when you run it using the Python interpreter. Storing your program code inside a Python source file saves you from having to retype it each time you want to tell the Python interpreter what to do.

As your programs get more complicated, however, you'll find that it becomes harder and harder to keep track of all the various functions and classes that you define. You'll forget where you put a particular piece of code and find it increasingly difficult to remember how all the various pieces fit together.

Modular programming is a way of organizing programs as they become more complicated. You can create a Python **module**, a source file that contains Python source code to do something useful, and then **import** this module into your program so that you can use it. For example, your program might need to keep track of various statistics about events that take place while the program is running. At the end, you might want to know how many events of each type have occurred. To achieve this, you might create a Python source file named `stats.py` which contains the following Python code:

```python
def init():
    global _stats
    _stats = {}

def event_occurred(event):
    global _stats
    try:
```

```
            _stats[event] = _stats[event] + 1
        except KeyError:
            _stats[event] = 1

    def get_stats():
        global _stats
        return sorted(_stats.items())
```

The `stats.py` Python source file defines a module named `stats` — as you can see, the name of the module is simply the name of the source file without the `.py` suffix. Your main program can make use of this module by importing it and then calling the various functions that you have defined as they are needed. The following frivolous example shows how you might use the `stats` module to collect and display statistics about events:

```
import stats

stats.init()
stats.event_occurred("meal_eaten")
stats.event_occurred("snack_eaten")
stats.event_occurred("meal_eaten")
stats.event_occurred("snack_eaten")
stats.event_occurred("meal_eaten")
stats.event_occurred("diet_started")
stats.event_occurred("meal_eaten")
stats.event_occurred("meal_eaten")
stats.event_occurred("meal_eaten")
stats.event_occurred("diet_abandoned")
stats.event_occurred("snack_eaten")

for event,num_times in stats.get_stats():
    print("{} occurred {} times".format(event, num_times))
```

We're not interested in recording meals and snacks, of course — this is just an example — but the important thing to notice here is how the `stats` module gets imported, and then how the various functions you defined within the `stats.py` file get used. For example, consider the following line of code:

```
stats.event_occurred("snack_eaten")
```

Because the `event_occurred()` function is defined within the `stats` module, you need to include the name of the module whenever you refer to this function.

There are ways in which you can import modules so you don't need to include the name of the module each time. We'll take a look at this in *Chapter 3, Using Modules and Packages*, when we look at namespaces and how the `import` command works in more detail.

As you can see, the `import` statement is used to load a module, and any time you see the module name followed by a period, you can tell that the program is referring to something (for example, a function or class) that is defined within that module.

Introducing Python packages

In the same way that Python modules allow you to organize your functions and classes into separate Python source files, Python **packages** allow you to group multiple modules together.

A Python package is a directory with certain characteristics. For example, consider the following directory of Python source files:

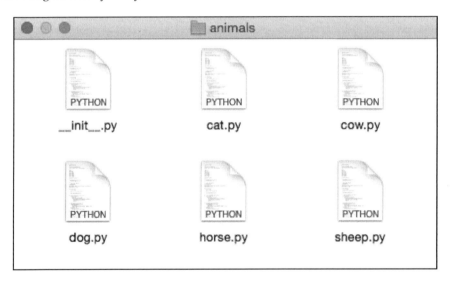

This Python package, called `animals`, contains five Python modules: `cat`, `cow`, `dog`, `horse`, and `sheep`. There is also a special file with the rather unusual name `__init__.py`. This file is called a **package initialization file**; the presence of this file tells the Python system that this directory contains a package. The package initialization file can also be used to initialize the package (hence the name) and can also be used to make importing the package easier.

> Starting with Python version 3.3, packages don't always need to include an initialization file. However, packages without an initialization file (called **namespace packages**) are still quite uncommon and are only used in very specific circumstances. To keep things simple, we will be using regular packages (with the `__init__.py` file) throughout this book.

Just like we used the module name when calling a function within a module, we use the package name when referring to a module within a package. For example, consider the following code:

```
import animals.cow
animals.cow.speak()
```

In this example, the `speak()` function is defined within the `cow.py` module, which itself is part of the `animals` package.

Packages are a great way of organizing more complicated Python programs. You can use them to group related modules together, and you can even define packages inside packages (called *nested packages*) to keep your program super-organized.

Note that the `import` statement (and the related `from...import` statement) can be used in a variety of ways to load packages and modules into your program. We have only scratched the surface here, showing you what modules and packages look like in Python so that you can recognize them when you see them in a program. We will be looking at the way modules and packages can be defined and imported in much more depth in *Chapter 3, Using Modules and Packages*.

Using modules and packages to organize a program

Modules and packages aren't just there to spread your Python code across multiple source files and directories—they allow you to *organize* your code to reflect the logical structure of what your program is trying to do. For example, imagine that you have been asked to create a web application to store and report on university examination results. Thinking about the business requirements that you have been given, you come up with the following overall structure for your application:

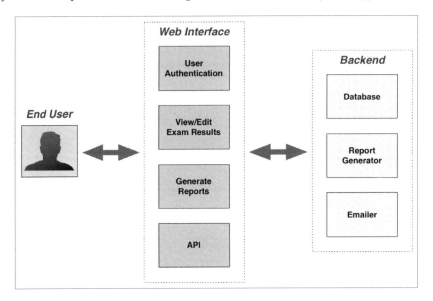

The program is broken into two main parts: a **web interface**, which interacts with the user (and with other computer programs via an API), and a **backend**, which handles the internal logic of storing information in a database, generating reports, and e-mailing results to students. As you can see, the web interface itself has been broken down into four parts:

- A user authentication section, which handles user sign-up, sign-in, and sign-out
- A web interface to view and enter exam results
- A web interface to generate reports
- An API, which allows other systems to retrieve exam results on request

As you consider each logical component of your application (that is, each of the boxes in the preceding illustration), you are also starting to think about the functionality that each component will provide. As you do this, you are already thinking in modular terms. Indeed, each of the logical components of your application can be directly implemented as a Python module or package. For example, you might choose to break your program into two main packages named web and backend, where:

- The web package has modules named authentication, results, reports, and api

- The backend package has modules named database, reportgenerator, and emailer

As you can see, each shaded box in the preceding illustration becomes a Python module, and each of the groupings of boxes becomes a Python package.

Once you have decided on the collection of packages and modules that you want to define, you can start to implement each component by writing the appropriate set of functions within each module. For example, the backend.database module might have a function named get_students_results(), which returns a single student's exam results for a given subject and year.

> In a real web application, your modular structure may actually be somewhat different. This is because you typically create a web application using a web application framework such as Django, which imposes its own structure on your program. However, in this example we are keeping the modular structure as simple as possible to show how business functionality translates directly into packages and modules.

Obviously, this example is fictitious, but it shows how you can think about a complex program in modular terms, breaking it down into individual components and then using Python modules and packages to implement each of these components in turn.

Why use modular programming techniques?

One of the great things about using modular design techniques, as opposed to just leaping in and writing code, is that they force you to think about the way your program should be structured and let you define a structure that will grow as your program evolves. Your program will be robust, easy to understand, easy to restructure as the scope of the program expands, and easy for others to work with too.

Woodworkers have a motto that equally applies to modular programming: there's a place for everything, and everything should be in its place. This is one of the hallmarks of high quality code, just as it's a hallmark of a well-organized woodworker's workshop.

To see why modular programming is such an important skill, imagine what would happen if you didn't apply modular techniques when writing a program. If you put all your Python code into a single source file, didn't try to logically arrange your functions and classes, and just randomly added new code to the end of the file, you would end up with a terrible mess of incomprehensible code. The following is an example of a program written without any sort of modular organization:

```python
import configparser

def load_config():
    config = configparser.ConfigParser()
    config.read("config.ini")
    return config['config']

def get_data_from_user():
    config = load_config()
    data = []
    for n in range(config.getint('num_data_points')):
        value = input("Data point {}: ".format(n+1))
        data.append(value)
    return data

def print_results(results):
    for value,num_times in results:
        print("{} = {}".format(value, num_times))

def analyze_data():
```

```
data = get_data_from_user()
results = {}
config = load_config()
for value in data:
    if config.getboolean('allow_duplicates'):
        try:
            results[value] = results[value] + 1
        except KeyError:
            results[value] = 1
    else:
        results[value] = 1
return results

def sort_results(results):
    sorted_results = []
    for value in results.keys():
        sorted_results.append((value, results[value]))
    sorted_results.sort()
    return sorted_results

if __name__ == "__main__":
    results = analyze_data()
    sorted_results = sort_results(results)
    print_results(sorted_results)
```

This program is intended to prompt the user for a number of data points and count how often each data point occurs. It does work, and the function and variable names do help to explain what each part of the program does—but it is still a mess. Just looking at the source code, it is hard to figure out what this program does. Functions were just added to the end of the file as the author decided to implement them, and even for a relatively small program, it is difficult to keep track of the various pieces. Imagine trying to debug or maintain a program like this if it was 10,000 lines long!

This program is an example of *spaghetti coding* — programming where everything is jumbled together and there is no overall organization to the source code. Unfortunately, spaghetti coding is often combined with other programming habits that make a program even harder to understand. Some of the more common problems include:

- Poorly chosen variable and function names that don't hint at what each variable or function is for. A typical example of this is a program that uses variable names such as a, b, c, and d.

- A complete lack of any documentation explaining what the code is supposed to do.

- Functions that have unexpected side effects. For example, imagine if the print_results() function in our example program modified the results array as it was being printed. If you wanted to print the results twice or use the results after they had been printed, your program would fail in a most mysterious way.

While modular programming won't cure all these ills, the fact that it forces you to think about the logical organization of your program will help you to avoid them. Organizing your code into logical pieces will help you structure your program so that you know where each part belongs. Thinking about the packages and modules, and what each module contains, will encourage you to choose clear and appropriate names for the various parts of your program. Using modules and packages also makes it natural to include **docstrings** to explain the functionality of each part of your program as you go along. Finally, using a logical structure encourages each part of your program to perform one particular task, reducing the likelihood of side effects creeping into your code.

Of course, like any programming technique, modular programming can be abused, but if it is used well it will vastly improve the quality of the programs you write.

Programming as a process

Imagine that you are writing a program to calculate the price of overseas purchases. Your company is based in England, and you need to calculate the local price of something purchased in US dollars. Someone else has already written a Python module which downloads the exchange rate, so your program starts out looking something like the following:

```
def calc_local_price(us_dollar_amount):
    exchange_rate = get_exchange_rate("USD", "EUR")
    local_amount = us_dollar_amount * exchange_rate
    return local_amount
```

So far so good. Your program is included in your company's online ordering system and the code goes into production. However, two months later, your company starts ordering products not just from the US, but from China, Germany, and Australia as well. You scramble to update your program to support these alternative currencies, and write something like the following:

```python
def calc_local_price(foreign_amount, from_country):
    if from_country == "United States":
        exchange_rate = get_exchange_rate("USD", "EUR")
    elif from_country == "China":
        exchange_rate = get_exchange_rate("CHN", "EUR")
    elif from_country == "Germany":
        exchange_rate = get_exchange_rate("EUR", "EUR")
    elif from_country = "Australia":
        exchange_rate = get_exchange_rate("AUS", "EUR")
    else:
        raise RuntimeError("Unsupported country: " + from_country)
    local_amount = us_dollar_amount * exchange_rate
    return local_amount
```

Once again, this program goes into production. Six months later, another 14 countries are added, and the project manager also decides to add a new feature, where the user can see how the price of a product has changed over time. As the programmer responsible for this code, you now have to add support for those 14 countries, and also add support for historical exchange rates going back in time.

This is a contrived example, of course, but it does show how programs typically evolve. Program code isn't something you write once and then leave forever. Your program is constantly changing and evolving in response to new requirements, newly discovered bugs, and unexpected consequences. Sometimes, a change that seems simple can be anything but. For example, consider the poor programmer who wrote the `get_exchange_rate()` function in our previous example. This function now has to support not only the current exchange rate for any given pair of currencies, it also has to return historical exchange rates going back to any desired point in time. If this function is obtaining its information from a source that doesn't support historical exchange rates, then the whole function may need to be rewritten from scratch to support an alternative data source.

Sometimes, programmers and IT managers try to suppress change, for example by writing detailed specifications and then implementing one part of the program at a time (the so-called *waterfall* method of programming). But change is an integral part of programming, and trying to suppress it is like trying to stop the wind from blowing—it's much better to just accept that your program *will* change, and learn how to manage the process as well as you can.

Modular techniques are an excellent way of managing change in your programs. For example, as your program grows and evolves, you may find that a particular change requires the addition of a new module to your program:

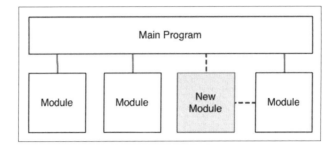

You can then import and use that module in the other parts of your program that need to use this new functionality.

Alternatively, you might find that a new feature only requires you to change the contents of a module:

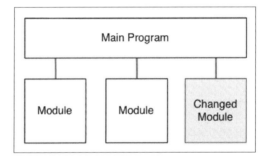

This is one of the major benefits of modular programming—since the details of how a particular feature is implemented is inside a module, you can often change the internals of a module without affecting any other parts of your program. The rest of your program continues to import and use the module as it did before—only the internal implementation of the module has changed.

Finally, you might find that you need to **refactor** your program. This is where you have to change the modular organization of your code to improve the way the program works:

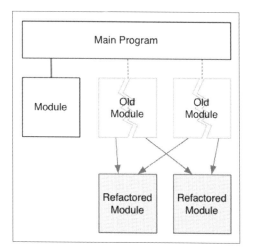

Refactoring may involve moving code between modules as well as creating new modules, removing old ones, and changing the way modules work. In essence, refactoring is the process of *rethinking* the program so that it works better.

In all of these changes, the use of modules and packages help you to manage the changes you make. Because the various modules and packages each perform a well-defined task, you know exactly which parts of your program need to be changed, and you can limit the effects of your changes to only the affected modules and the parts of the system that use them.

Modular programming won't make change go away, but it will help you to deal with change—and the ongoing process of programming—in the best possible way.

The Python Standard Library

One of the buzzwords used to describe Python is that it is a *batteries included* language, that is, it comes with a rich collection of built-in modules and packages called the **Python Standard Library**. If you've written any non-trivial Python program, you've almost certainly used modules from the Python Standard Library to do so. To get an idea of how vast the Python Standard Library is, here are a few example modules from this library:

Module	Description
datetime	Defines classes to store and perform calculations using date and time values
tempfile	Defines a range of functions to work with temporary files and directories
csv	Supports reading and writing of CSV format files
hashlib	Implements cryptographically secure hashes
logging	Allows you to write log messages and manage log files
threading	Supports multi-threaded programming
html	A collection of modules (that is, a package) used to parse and generate HTML documents
unittest	A framework for creating and running unit tests
urllib	A collection of modules to read data from URLs

These are just a few of the over 300 modules available in the Python Standard Library. As you can see, there is a vast range of functionality provided, and all of this is built in to every Python distribution.

Because of the huge range of functionality provided, the Python Standard Library is an excellent example of modular programming. For example, the `math` standard library module provides a range of mathematical functions that make it easier to work with integer and floating-point numbers. If you look through the documentation for this module (`http://docs.python.org/3/library/math.html`), you will find a large collection of functions and constants, all defined within the `math` module, that perform almost any mathematical operation you could imagine. In this example, the various functions and constants are all defined within a single module, making it easy to refer to them when you need to.

In contrast, the xmlrpc package allows you to make and respond to remote procedure calls that use the XML protocol to send and receive data. The xmlrpc package is made up of two modules: xmlrpc.server and xmlrpc.client, where the server module allows you to create an XML-RPC server, and the client module includes code to access and use an XML-RPC server. This is an example of where a hierarchy of modules is used to logically group related functionality together (in this case, within the xmlrpc package), while using sub-modules to separate out the particular parts of the package.

If you haven't already done so, it is worth spending some time to review the documentation for the Python Standard Library. This can be found at https://docs.python.org/3/library/. It is worth studying this documentation to see how Python has organized such a vast collection of features into modules and packages.

The Python Standard Library is not perfect, but it has been improved over time, and the library as it is today makes a great example of modular programming techniques applied to a comprehensive library, covering a wide range of features and functions.

Creating your first module

Now that we've seen what modules are and how they can be used, let's implement our first real Python module. While this module is simple, you may find it a useful addition to the programs you write.

Caching

In computer programming, a **cache** is a way of storing previously calculated results so that they can be retrieved more quickly. For example, imagine that your program had to calculate shipping costs based on three parameters:

- The weight of the ordered item
- The dimensions of the ordered item
- The customer's location

Calculating the shipping cost based on the customer's location might be quite involved. For example, you may have a fixed charge for deliveries within your city but charge a premium for out-of-town orders based on how far away the customer is. You may even need to send a query to a freight company's API to see how much it will charge to ship the given item.

Since the process of calculating the shipping cost can be quite complex and time consuming, it makes sense to use a cache to store the previously calculated results. This allows you to use the previously calculated results rather than having to recalculate the shipping cost each time. To do this, you would need to structure your `calc_shipping_cost()` function to look something like the following:

```
def calc_shipping_cost(params):
    if params in cache:
        shipping_cost = cache[params]
    else:
        ...calculate the shipping cost.
        cache[params] = shipping_cost
    return shipping_cost
```

As you can see, we take the supplied parameters (in this case, the weight, dimensions, and the customer's location) and check whether there is already an entry in the cache for those parameters. If so, we retrieve the previously-calculated shipping cost from the cache. Otherwise, we go through the possibly time-consuming process of calculating the shipping cost, storing this in the cache using the supplied parameters, and then returning the shipping cost back to the caller.

Notice how the `cache` variable in the preceding pseudo code looks very much like a Python dictionary—you can store entries in the dictionary based on a given key and then retrieve the entry using this key. There is, however, a crucial difference between a dictionary and a cache: a cache typically has a *limit* on the number of entries that it can contain, while the dictionary has no such limit. This means that a dictionary will continue to grow forever, possibly taking up all the computer's memory if the program runs for a long time, while a cache will never take too much memory, as the number of entries is limited.

Once the cache reaches its maximum size, an existing entry has to be removed each time a new entry is added so that the cache doesn't continue to grow:

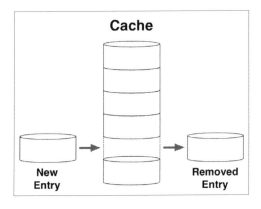

While there are various ways of choosing the entry to remove, the most common way is to remove the least recently used entry, that is, the entry that hasn't been used for the longest period of time.

Caches are very commonly used in computer programs. In fact, even if you haven't yet used a cache in the programs you write, you've almost certainly encountered them before. Has someone ever suggested that you *clear your browser's cache* to solve a problem with your web browser? Yes, web browsers use a cache to hold previously downloaded images and web pages so that they don't have to be retrieved again, and clearing the contents of the browser cache is a common way of fixing a misbehaving web browser.

Writing a cache module

Let's now write our own Python module to implement a cache. Before we write it, let's think about the functionality that our cache module will require:

- We're going to limit the size of our cache to 100 entries.
- We will need an `init()` function to initialize the cache.
- We will have a `set(key, value)` function to store an entry in the cache.
- A `get(key)` function will retrieve an entry from the cache. If there is no entry for that key, this function should return `None`.
- We'll also need a `contains(key)` function to check whether a given entry is in the cache.
- Finally, we'll implement a `size()` function which returns the number of entries in the cache.

 We are deliberately keeping the implementation of this module quite simple. A real cache would make use of a `Cache` class to allow you to use multiple caches at once. It would also allow the size of the cache to be configured as necessary. To keep things simple, however, we will implement these functions directly within a module, as we want to concentrate on modular programming rather than combining it with object-oriented programming and other techniques.

Go ahead and create a new Python source file named `cache.py`. This file will hold the Python source code for our new module. At the top of this module, enter the following Python code:

```
import datetime

MAX_CACHE_SIZE = 100
```

We will be using the `datetime` Standard Library module to calculate the least recently used entry in the cache. The second statement, defining MAX_CACHE SIZE, sets the maximum size for our cache.

 Note that we are following the standard Python convention of defining constants using uppercase letters. This makes them easier to see in your source code.

We now want to implement the `init()` function for our cache. To do this, add the following to the end of your module:

```
def init():
    global _cache
    _cache = {} # Maps key to (datetime, value) tuple.
```

As you can see, we have created a new function named `init()`. The first statement in this function, `global _cache`, defines a new variable named `_cache`. The `global` statement makes this variable available as a *module-level global variable*, that is, this variable can be shared by all parts of the `cache.py` module.

Notice the underscore character at the start of the variable name. In Python, a leading underscore is a convention indicating that a name is private. In other words, the `_cache` global is intended to be used as an internal part of the `cache.py` module — the underscore tells you that you shouldn't need to use this variable outside of the `cache.py` module itself.

The second statement in the `init()` function sets the `_cache` global to an empty dictionary. Notice that we've added a comment explaining how the dictionary will be used; it's good practice to add notes like this to your code so others (and you, when you look at this code after a long time working on something else) can easily see what this variable is used for.

In summary, calling the `init()` function has the effect of creating a private `_cache` variable within the module and setting it to an empty dictionary. Let's now write the `set()` function, which will use this variable to store an entry in the cache.

Add the following to the end of your module:

```
def set(key, value):
    global _cache
    if key not in _cache and len(_cache) >= MAX_CACHE_SIZE:
        _remove_oldest_entry()
    _cache[key] = [datetime.datetime.now(), value]
```

Once again, the `set()` function starts with a `global _cache` statement. This makes the `_cache` module-level global variable available for the function to use.

The `if` statement checks to see whether the cache is going to exceed the maximum allowed size. If so, we call a new function, named `_remove_oldest_entry()`, to remove the oldest entry from the cache. Notice how this function name also starts with an underscore—once again, this indicates that this function is private and should only be used by code within the module itself.

Finally, we store the entry in the `_cache` dictionary. Notice that we store the current date and time as well as the value in the cache; this will let us know when the cache entry was last used, which is important when we have to remove the oldest entry.

Let's now implement the `get()` function. Add the following to the end of your module:

```
def get(key):
    global _cache
    if key in _cache:
        _cache[key][0] = datetime.datetime.now()
        return _cache[key][1]
    else:
        return None
```

You should be able to figure out what this code does. The only interesting part to note is that we update the date and time for the cache entry before returning the associated value. This lets us know when the cache entry was last used.

With these functions implemented, the remaining two functions should also be easy to understand. Add the following to the end of your module:

```
def contains(key):
    global _cache
    return key in _cache

def size():
    global _cache
    return len(_cache)
```

There shouldn't be any surprises here.

There's only one more function left to implement: our private `_remove_oldest_entry()` function. Add the following to the end of your module:

```
def _remove_oldest_entry():
    global _cache
    oldest = None
```

```
        for key in _cache.keys():
            if oldest == None:
                oldest = key
            elif _cache[key][0] < _cache[oldest][0]:
                oldest = key
        if oldest != None:
            del _cache[oldest]
```

This completes the implementation of our `cache.py` module itself, with the five main functions we described earlier, as well as one private function and one private global variable which are used internally to help implement our public functions.

Using the cache

Let's now write a simple test program to use this `cache` module and verify that it's working properly. Create a new Python source file, which we'll call `test_cache.py`, and add the following to this file:

```
import random
import string
import cache

def random_string(length):
    s = ''
    for i in range(length):
        s = s + random.choice(string.ascii_letters)
    return s

cache.init()

for n in range(1000):
    while True:
        key = random_string(20)
        if cache.contains(key):
            continue
        else:
            break
    value = random_string(20)
    cache.set(key, value)
    print("After {} iterations, cache has {} entries".format(n+1,
cache.size()))
```

This program starts by importing three modules: two from the Python Standard Library, and the `cache` module we have just written. We then define a utility function named `random_string()`, which generates a string of random letters of a given length. After this, we initialize the cache by calling `cache.init()` and then generate 1,000 random entries to add to the cache. After adding each cache entry, we print out the number of entries we have added as well as the current cache size.

If you run this program, you can see that it's working as expected:

```
$ python test_cache.py
After 1 iterations, cache has 1 entries
After 2 iterations, cache has 2 entries
After 3 iterations, cache has 3 entries
...
After 98 iterations, cache has 98 entries
After 99 iterations, cache has 99 entries
After 100 iterations, cache has 100 entries
After 101 iterations, cache has 100 entries
After 102 iterations, cache has 100 entries
...
After 998 iterations, cache has 100 entries
After 999 iterations, cache has 100 entries
After 1000 iterations, cache has 100 entries
```

The cache continues to grow until it reaches 100 entries, at which point the oldest entry is removed to make room for a new one. This ensures that the cache stays the same size, no matter how many new entries are added.

While there is a lot more we could do with our `cache.py` module, this is enough to demonstrate how to create a useful Python module and then use it within another program. Of course, you aren't just limited to importing modules within a main program — modules can import other modules as well.

Summary

In this chapter, we introduced the concept of Python modules and saw how Python modules are simply Python source files, which are imported and used by another source file. We then took a look at Python packages and saw that these are collections of modules identified by a package initialization file named `__init__.py`.

We explored how modules and packages can be used to organize your program's source code and why the use of these modular techniques is so important for the development of large systems. We also explored what spaghetti code looks like and discovered some of the other pitfalls that can occur if you don't modularize your programs.

Next, we looked at programming as a process of constant change and evolution and how modular programming can help deal with a changing codebase in the best possible way. We then learned that the Python Standard Library is an excellent example of a large collection of modules and packages, and finished by creating our own simple Python module that demonstrates effective modular programming techniques. In implementing this module, we learned how a module can use leading underscores in variable and function names to mark them as *private* to the module, while making the remaining functions and other definitions available for other parts of the system to use.

In the next chapter, we will apply modular techniques to the development of a more sophisticated program consisting of several modules working together to solve a more complex programming problem.

2

Writing Your First Modular Program

In this chapter, we will use modular programming techniques to implement a nontrivial program. Along the way, we will:

- Learn about the *divide and conquer* approach to program design

- Examine the tasks our program needs to perform

- Look at the information our program will need to store

- Apply modular techniques to break our program down into individual parts

- Figure out how each part can be implemented as a separate Python module

- See how the various modules work together to implement our program's functionality

- Follow this process to implement a simple but complete inventory control system

- See how modular techniques allow you to add functionality to your program while minimizing the changes that need to be made

The inventory control system

Imagine that you have been asked to write a program that allows the user to keep track of the company's inventory—that is, the various items the company has available for sale. For each inventory item, you have been asked to keep track of the product code and the item's current location. New items will be added as they are received, and existing items will be removed once they have been sold. Your program will also need to generate two types of reports: a report listing the company's current inventory, including how many of each type of item there are in each location, and a report that is used to re-order inventory items once they have been sold.

Looking at these requirements, it is clear that there are three different types of information that we will need to store:

1. A list of the different types of **products** that the company has for sale. For each product type, we will need to know the **product code** (sometimes called an SKU number), a **description**, and the **desired number of items** that the company should have in its inventory for that type of product.

2. A list of the **locations** where inventory items can be held. These locations might be individual shops, warehouses, or storerooms. Alternatively, a location might identify a particular shelf or aisle within a shop. For each location, we need to have a **location code** and a **description** identifying that location.

3. Finally, a list of the **inventory items** that the company currently holds. Each inventory item has a **product code** and a **location code**; these identify the type of product and where the item is currently held.

When running the program, the end user should be able to perform the following actions:

- Add a new item to the inventory
- Remove an item from the inventory
- Generate a report of the current inventory items
- Generate a report of the inventory items that need to be re-ordered
- Quit the program

While this program is not too complicated, there are enough features here to benefit from a modular design, while still keeping our discussion relatively brief. Now that we have taken a look at what our program needs to do and the information we need to store, let's start applying modular programming techniques to the design of our system.

Designing the inventory control system

If you step back and review our inventory control program's functionality, you can see that there are three fundamental types of activity that this program needs to support:

- Storing information
- Interacting with the user
- Generating reports

While this is very general, this breakdown is helpful because it suggests a possible way of organizing our program code. For example, the part of the system responsible for storing information could store the lists of products, locations, and inventory items and make this information available as required. Similarly, the part of the system responsible for interacting with the user could prompt the user to choose an action to perform, ask them to select a product code, and so on. Finally, the area of the system responsible for generating reports would be able to generate each of the desired types of report.

Thinking about the system in this way, it becomes clear that each of these three *parts* of the system could be implemented as a separate module:

- The part of the system responsible for storing information could be called the **data storage** module
- The part of the system responsible for interacting with the user could be called the **user interface** module
- The part of the system responsible for generating reports could be called the **report generator** module

As the names suggest, each of these modules perform a particular purpose. In addition to these special-purpose modules, we are going to need one more part to our system: a Python source file that the user executes to start up and run the inventory control system. Because this is the part the user actually runs, we will call this the **main program**, which is often stored in a Python source file named `main.py`.

We now have four parts to our system: three modules plus a main program. Each of these parts will have a particular job to do, and the various parts will often interact to perform a particular function. For example, the report generator module will need to obtain a list of the available product codes from the data storage module. These various interactions are represented by arrows in the following diagram:

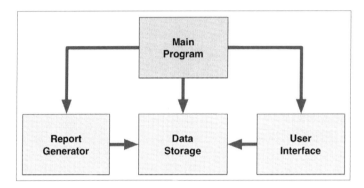

Now that we have an idea of the overall structure for our program, let's take a closer look at each of these four parts to see how they will work.

The data storage module

This module will be responsible for storing all of our program's data. We already know that we'll need to store three types of information: a list of **products**, a list of **locations**, and a list of **inventory items**.

To keep our program as simple as possible, we will make two major design decisions regarding the data storage module:

- The lists of products and locations will be hardwired into our program
- We will hold the list of inventory items in memory and save it to disk whenever the list changes

A more sophisticated implementation of our inventory control system would store this information in a database and allow the user to view and edit the lists of product codes and locations. In our case, however, we are more interested in the overall structure of our program, so we want to keep the implementation as simple as possible.

While the list of product codes will be hardwired, we don't necessarily want to build this list into the data storage module itself. The data storage module is responsible for storing and retrieving information—it isn't the data storage module's job to define the list of product codes. Because of this, we are going to need a function within the data storage module that can be called to set the list of product codes. This function will look like the following:

```
def set_products(products):
    ...
```

We've already decided that for each product, we want to store the **product code**, a **description**, and the **desired number of items** that the user wants to keep in their inventory for that type of product. To support this, we're going to define the list of products (as supplied in the `products` parameter to our `set_products()` function) as a list of (`code, description, desired_number`) tuples. For example, our list of products might look something like this:

```
[("CODE01", "Product 1", 10),
 ("CODE02", "Product 2", 200), ...
]
```

Once the list of products have been defined, we can provide a function to return this list as needed:

```
def products():
    ...
```

This would simply return the list of products, allowing your code to work with this list as needed. For example, you can scan through the list of products using the following Python code:

```
for code,description,desired_number in products():
    ...
```

These two functions allow us to define the (hardwired) list of products and retrieve this list whenever we need it. Let's now define the equivalent two functions for the list of locations.

First, we need a function to set the hardwired list of locations:

```
def set_locations(locations):
    ...
```

Each item in the `locations` list will be a (`code, description`) tuple, where `code` is the code for a location and `description` is a string describing the location so that the user knows where it is.

We then need a function to retrieve this list of locations as needed:

```
def locations():
    ...
```

Once again, this returns the list of locations, allowing us to work with these locations as required.

We now need to decide on how the data storage module will allow the user to store and retrieve the list of inventory items. An inventory item is defined as a product code plus a location code. In other words, an inventory item is a particular type of product at a particular location.

To retrieve the list of inventory items, we'll use the following function:

```
def items():
    ...
```

Following the design we used for the `products()` and `locations()` functions, the `items()` function will return a list of the inventory items, where each inventory item is a `(product_code, location_code)` tuple.

Unlike the lists of products and locations, however, the list of inventory items will not be hardwired: the user will be able to add and remove inventory items. To support this, we're going to need two more functions:

```
def add_item(product_code, location_code):
    ...


def remove_item(product_code, location_code):
    ...
```

There is only one more part of our data storage module that we need to design: since we know that we'll be storing the list of inventory items in memory and saving them to disk as required, we're going to need some way of loading the inventory items from disk into memory when the program starts. To support this, we're going to define an **initialization function** for our module:

```
def init():
    ...
```

We've now decided on a total of eight functions for the data storage module. These eight functions make up the **public interface** for our module. In other words, the other parts of the system will *only* interact with our module using these eight functions:

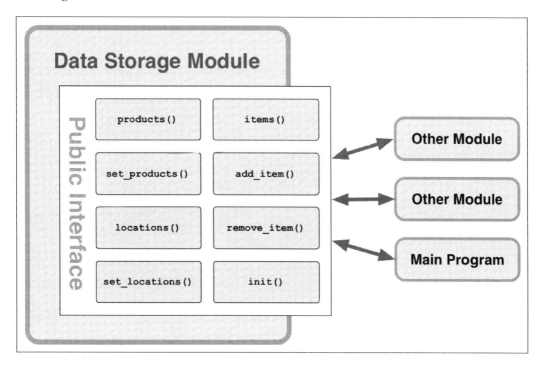

Notice the process we went through here: we started by looking at what our module needed to do (in this case, storing and retrieving information) and then designed the module's public interface based on those requirements. For the first seven functions, we used our business requirements to help us design the interface, while for the final function, init(), we used our knowledge of how the module will work internally to change the interface so that the module can do its job. This is a common way of working: both the business requirements and the technical requirements will help shape the module's interface and how it interacts with the rest of the system.

Now that we've designed our data storage module, let's repeat the process for the other modules in our system.

The user interface module

The user interface module will be responsible for interacting with the user. This includes asking the user for information, as well as displaying information on the screen. To keep things simple, we will use a simple text-based interface for our inventory control system, using `print()` statements to display information and `input()` to ask the user to enter something.

A more sophisticated implementation of our inventory control system would use a graphical user interface with windows, menus, and dialog boxes. Doing this would make the inventory control system much more complicated and is well beyond the scope of what we are trying to achieve here. However, because of the modular design of the system, if we were to rewrite the user interface to use menus, windows, and the like, we would only be changing this one module—the rest of the system would be unaffected.

> This is actually a slight oversimplification. Replacing a text-based interface with a GUI requires many changes to the system, and would probably require us to change the module's public functions slightly, just like we had to add an `init()` function to the data storage module to allow for the way it worked internally. However, because of the modular way we're designing our system, the other modules would not be affected if we rewrote the user interface module to use a GUI.

Let's think about the various tasks our inventory control system needs to perform from the point of view of the user's interaction with the system:

1. The user needs to be able to select an action to perform.
2. When the user wants to add a new inventory item, we need to prompt the user for the details of the new item.
3. When the user wants to remove an inventory item, we need to prompt the user for the details of the inventory item to remove.
4. When the user wishes to generate a report, we need to be able to display the contents of the report to the user.

Let's work through these interactions one at a time:

1. To select an action to perform, we'll have a `prompt_for_action()` function which returns a string identifying the action that the user wishes to perform. Let's define the codes that this function can return for the various actions the user can perform:

Action	Action code
Add an inventory item	ADD
Remove an inventory item	REMOVE
Generate a report of the current inventory items	INVENTORY_REPORT
Generate a report of the inventory items that need to be re-ordered	REORDER_REPORT
Quit the program	QUIT

2. To add an inventory item, the user will need to be prompted for the details of the new item. Because an inventory item is defined as a given product at a given location, we actually need to prompt the user to choose both the product and the location for the new item. To prompt the user to select a product, we will use the following function:

```
def prompt_for_product():
    ...
```

The user will be shown a list of the available products and then choose an item from the list. If they cancel, `prompt_for_product()` will return None. Otherwise, it will return the product code for the selected product.

Similarly, to prompt the user to select a location, we will define the following function:

```
def prompt_for_location():
    ...
```

Once again, this displays a list of the available locations, and the user can choose a location from the list. If they cancel, we return None. Otherwise, we return the location code for the selected location.

Using these two functions, we can ask the user to identify a new inventory item, and then we use the data storage module's `add_item()` function to add it to the list.

3. Because we are implementing this as a simple text-based system, the process of removing an inventory item is almost identical to the process used to add an item: the user will be prompted for the product and location, and the inventory item at that location will be removed. Because of this, we won't need any additional functions to implement this feature.

4. To generate a report, we will simply call the report generator module to do the work, and then we display the resulting report to the user. To keep things simple, our reports won't take any parameters, and the resulting report will be displayed in plain-text format. Because of this, the only user interface function that we will need is a function to display the plain-text contents of the report:

```
def show_report(report):
    ...
```

The `report` parameter will simply be a list of strings containing the generated report. All the `show_report()` function needs to do is print out these strings, one at a time, to show the contents of the report to the user.

This completes our design for the user interface module. There are a total of four public functions which we will need to implement for this module.

The report generator module

The report generator module is responsible for generating reports. Since there are two types of report that we need to be able to generate, we are simply going to have two public functions in the report generator module, one for each type of report:

```
def generate_inventory_report():
    ...

def generate_reorder_report():
    ...
```

Each of these functions will generate a report of the given type, returning the report's contents as a list of strings. Note that there are no parameters to these functions; because we are keeping things as simple as possible, the reports won't use any parameters to control how they are to be generated.

The main program

The main program isn't a module. Instead, it is a standard Python source file that the user runs to start the system. The main program will import the various modules it needs, and call the functions we have defined to do all the work. In a sense, our main program is the glue that binds together all the other parts of the system.

In Python, when a source file is intended to be run (as opposed to being imported and used by other modules or from the Python command line), it is common to use the following structure for the source file:

```
def main():
    ...

if __name__ == "__main__":
    main()
```

All of the program's logic is written inside the `main()` function, which is then called by the final two lines in the file. The `if __name__ == "__main__"` line is a piece of Python magic that basically means *if this program is being run*. In other words, if the user is running this program, call the `main()` function to do all the work.

> We could put all the program's logic beneath the `if __name__ == "__main__"` statement, but there are some advantages to putting our program's logic in a separate function. By using a separate function, we can simply return from this function when we want to exit. It also makes error handling easier, and the code is better organized because our main program code is separate from the code that checks whether we are actually running the program.

We are going to use this design for our main program, putting all the actual functionality within a single function called `main()`.

Our `main()` function is going to do the following:

1. Call the `init()` function for the various modules which need to be initialized.
2. Provide the hardwired lists of products and locations.
3. Ask the user interface module to prompt the user for a command.
4. Respond to the command entered by the user.

Steps 3 and 4 will be repeated indefinitely until the user quits.

Implementing the inventory control system

Now that we have a good idea of the overall structure for our system, what our various modules will be, and what functionality they will provide, it's time for us to start implementing the system. Let's start with the data storage module.

Implementing the data storage module

Create a directory somewhere convenient where you can store the source code for the inventory control system. You might want to call this directory `inventoryControl` or something similar.

Inside this directory, we will place our various modules and files. Start by creating a new, empty Python source file named `datastorage.py`. This Python source file will hold our data storage module.

 When selecting the name for our modules, we are following the Python convention of using all lowercase letters. You might find this a bit awkward at first, but it soon becomes easy to read. Please refer to `https://www.python.org/dev/peps/pep-0008/#package-and-module-names` for more information about these naming conventions.

We already know that we are going to need eight different functions to make up the public interface to this module, so go ahead and add the following Python code to this module:

```python
def init():
    pass

def items():
    pass

def products():
    pass

def locations():
    pass

def add_item(product_code, location_code):
    pass

def remove_item(product_code, location_code):
```

```
        pass

    def set_products(products):
        pass

    def set_locations(locations):
        pass
```

The `pass` statements allow us to leave the functions empty—these are just placeholders for the code we are going to write.

Let's now implement the `init()` function. This initializes the data storage module when the system is run. Because we are holding the list of inventory items in memory and saving them to disk when they change, our `init()` function is going to have to load the inventory items from a file on disk back into memory so that they will be available when we need them. To do this, we'll define a private function, which we'll call `_load_items()`, and call this from our `init()` function.

 Remember that a leading underscore means that something is private. This means that the `_load_items()` function won't be part of the public interface for our module.

Change your definition of the `init()` function to look like the following:

```
    def init():
        _load_items()
```

The `_load_items()` function is going to load the list of inventory items from a file on disk into a private global variable, which we'll call `_items`. Let's go ahead and implement this function now, by adding the following to the end of the module:

```
    def _load_items():
        global _items
        if os.path.exists("items.json"):
            f = open("items.json", "r")
            _items = json.loads(f.read())
            f.close()
        else:
            _items = []
```

Notice that we store the list of inventory items in a file named `items.json`, and that we are using the `json` module to convert the `_items` list from a text file into a Python list.

JSON is an excellent way of saving and loading Python data structures, and the resulting text file is easy to read. Since the json module is built into the Python Standard Library, we might as well make use of it.

Because we are now using some modules from the Python Standard Library, you'll need to add the following import statements to the top of your module:

```
import json
import os.path
```

While we're at it, let's write a function to save the list of inventory items to disk. Add the following to the end of your module:

```
def _save_items():
    global _items
    f = open("items.json", "w")
    f.write(json.dumps(_items))
    f.close()
```

Since we have loaded the list of inventory items into a private global variable named _items, we can now implement the items() function to make this data available. Edit your definition of the items() function to look like the following:

```
def items():
    global _items
    return _items
```

Let's now implement the add_item() and remove_item() functions to let the rest of the system manipulate our list of inventory items. Edit these functions so they look like the following:

```
def add_item(product_code, location_code):
    global _items
    _items.append((product_code, location_code))
    _save_items()

def remove_item(product_code, location_code):
    global _items
    for i in range(len(_items)):
        prod_code, loc_code = _items[i]
        if prod_code == product_code and loc_code == location_code:
            del _items[i]
            _save_items()
            return True
    return False
```

Notice that the `remove_item()` function returns `True` if the item was successfully removed and `False` otherwise; this tells the rest of the system if an attempt to remove an inventory item was successful or not.

We've now implemented all the functions within the `datastorage` module that relate to inventory items. Next, we'll implement the product-related functions.

Since we know we're going to hardwire the list of products, the `set_products()` function is going to be trivial:

```
def set_products(products):
    global _products
    _products = products
```

We simply store the list of products in a private global variable named `_products`. We can then make this list available via the `products()` function:

```
def products():
    global _products
    return _products
```

Similarly, we can now implement the `set_locations()` function to set the hardwired list of locations:

```
def set_locations(locations):
    global _locations
    _locations = locations
```

Finally, we can implement the `locations()` function to make this information available:

```
def locations():
    global _locations
    return _locations
```

This completes our implementation of the `datastorage` module.

Implementing the user interface module

As mentioned earlier, the user interface module is going to be kept as simple as possible, using `print()` and `input()` statements to interact with the user. In a more comprehensive implementation of this system, we would use a graphical user interface (GUI) to display and ask the user for information, but we want to keep our code as simple as we can.

With this in mind, let's go ahead and implement the first of our user interface module functions. Create a new Python source file named userinterface.py to hold our user interface module, and add the following to this file:

```python
def prompt_for_action():
    while True:
        print()
        print("What would you like to do?")
        print()
        print("  A = add an item to the inventory.")
        print("  R = remove an item from the inventory.")
        print("  C = generate a report of the current inventory
levels.")
        print("  O = generate a report of the inventory items to re-
order.")
        print("  Q = quit.")
        print()
        action = input("> ").strip().upper()
        if    action == "A": return "ADD"
        elif action == "R": return "REMOVE"
        elif action == "C": return "INVENTORY_REPORT"
        elif action == "O": return "REORDER_REPORT"
        elif action == "Q": return "QUIT"
        else:
            print("Unknown action!")
```

As you can see, we prompt the user to type a letter corresponding to each action, displaying the list of available actions and returning a string which identifies the action the user selected. This is not a great way of implementing a user interface, but it works.

The next function we want to implement is prompt_for_product(), which asks the user to select a product from the list of available product codes. To do this, we are going to have to ask the data storage module for the list of products. Add the following code to the end of your userinterface.py module:

```python
def prompt_for_product():
    while True:
        print()
        print("Select a product:")
        print()
        n = 1
        for code,description,desired_number in datastorage.products():
            print("  {}. {} - {}".format(n, code, description))
```

```
        n = n + 1

    s = input("> ").strip()
    if s == "": return None

    try:
        n = int(s)
    except ValueError:
        n = -1

    if n < 1 or n > len(datastorage.products()):
        print("Invalid option: {}".format(s))
        continue

    product_code = datastorage.products()[n-1][0]
    return product_code
```

In this function, we display a list of the products along with a number beside each product. The user then enters the number for the desired product, and we return the product code to the caller. If the user didn't enter anything, we return None — this lets the user press the *Enter* key without entering anything if they don't want to proceed.

While we're at it, let's implement the equivalent function which asks the user to identify a location:

```
def prompt_for_location():
    while True:
        print()
        print("Select a location:")
        print()
        n = 1
        for code,description in datastorage.locations():
            print("  {}. {} - {}".format(n, code, description))
            n = n + 1

        s = input("> ").strip()
        if s == "": return None

        try:
            n = int(s)
        except ValueError:
            n = -1

        if n < 1 or n > len(datastorage.locations()):
```

```
        print("Invalid option: {}".format(s))
        continue

    location_code = datastorage.locations()[n-1][0]
    return location_code
```

Once again, this function displays a number beside each location and asks the user to enter the number for the desired location. We then return the location code for the selected location, or None if the user cancelled.

Since these two functions make use of the data storage module, we're going to have to add the following import statement to the top of our module:

```
import datastorage
```

There is only one more function we need to implement: the show_report() function. Let's do this now:

```
def show_report(report):
    print()
    for line in report:
        print(line)
    print()
```

Since we are implementing this using a text interface, this function is almost ludicrously simple. It does serve an important purpose though: by implementing the process of showing a report as a separate function, we can re-implement this function to show the report in a more useful way (for example, displaying it in a window within a GUI) without affecting the rest of the system.

Implementing the report generator module

The report generator module is going to have two public functions, one to generate each type of report. Without further ado, let's implement this module, which we will store in a Python source file named reportgenerator.py. Create this file, and enter the following into it:

```
import datastorage

def generate_inventory_report():
    product_names = {}
    for product_code,name,desired_number in datastorage.products():
        product_names[product_code] = name

    location_names = {}
```

```
    for location_code,name in datastorage.locations():
        location_names[location_code] = name


    grouped_items = {}
    for product_code,location_code in datastorage.items():
        if product_code not in grouped_items:
            grouped_items[product_code] = {}


        if location_code not in grouped_items[product_code]:
            grouped_items[product_code][location_code] = 1
        else:
            grouped_items[product_code][location_code] += 1


    report = []
    report.append("INVENTORY REPORT")
    report.append("")


    for product_code in sorted(grouped_items.keys()):
        product_name = product_names[product_code]
        report.append("Inventory for product: {} - {}"
                    .format(product_code, product_name))
        report.append("")


        for location_code in sorted(grouped_items[product_code].
keys()):
            location_name = location_names[location_code]
            num_items = grouped_items[product_code][location_code]
            report.append("  {} at {} - {}"
                        .format(num_items,
                                location_code,
                                location_name))
        report.append("")


    return report



def generate_reorder_report():
    product_names   = {}
    desired_numbers = {}


    for product_code,name,desired_number in datastorage.products():
        product_names[product_code] = name
```

```
        desired_numbers[product_code] = desired_number

    num_in_inventory = {}
    for product_code,location_code in datastorage.items():
        if product_code in num_in_inventory:
            num_in_inventory[product_code] += 1
        else:
            num_in_inventory[product_code] = 1

    report = []
    report.append("RE-ORDER REPORT")
    report.append("")

    for product_code in sorted(product_names.keys()):
        desired_number = desired_numbers[product_code]
        current_number = num_in_inventory.get(product_code, 0)
        if current_number < desired_number:
            product_name = product_names[product_code]
            num_to_reorder = desired_number - current_number
            report.append("  Re-order {} of {} - {}"
                        .format(num_to_reorder,
                                product_code,
                                product_name))
    report.append("")

    return report
```

Don't worry too much about the details of these functions. As you can see, we take the list of inventory items, the list of products, and the list of locations from the data storage module, and generate a simple text-based report based on the contents of these lists.

Implementing the main program

The final part of the system we need to implement is our main program. Create another Python source file named main.py, and enter the following into this file:

```
import datastorage
import userinterface
import reportgenerator

def main():
```

```
    pass

if __name__ == "__main__":
    main()
```

This is just the overall template for our main program: we import the various modules we created, define a `main()` function where all the work will be done, and call it when the program is run. We now need to write our `main()` function.

Our first task is to initialize the other modules and define the hardwired lists of products and locations. Let's do this now, by rewriting our `main()` function to look like the following:

```
def main():
    datastorage.init()

    datastorage.set_products([
        ("SKU123", "4 mm flat-head wood screw",         50),
        ("SKU145", "6 mm flat-head wood screw",         50),
        ("SKU167", "4 mm countersunk head wood screw", 10),
        ("SKU169", "6 mm countersunk head wood screw", 10),
        ("SKU172", "4 mm metal self-tapping screw",     20),
        ("SKU185", "8 mm metal self-tapping screw",     20),
    ])

    datastorage.set_locations([
        ("S1A1", "Shelf 1, Aisle 1"),
        ("S2A1", "Shelf 2, Aisle 1"),
        ("S3A1", "Shelf 3, Aisle 1"),
        ("S1A2", "Shelf 1, Aisle 2"),
        ("S2A2", "Shelf 2, Aisle 2"),
        ("S3A2", "Shelf 3, Aisle 2"),
        ("BIN1", "Storage Bin 1"),
        ("BIN2", "Storage Bin 2"),
    ])
```

Next, we need to ask the user for the action they wish to perform, and then respond appropriately. We'll start by asking the user for the action, using a `while` statement so that this can be done repeatedly:

```
    while True:
        action = userinterface.prompt_for_action()
```

We next need to respond to the action that the user selected. Obviously, we need to do this for each possible action. Let's start with the QUIT action:

```
if action == "QUIT":
    break
```

The break statement will exit the while True statement, which has the effect of leaving the main() function and shutting down the program.

Next, we want to implement the ADD action:

```
elif action == "ADD":
    product = userinterface.prompt_for_product()
    if product != None:
        location = userinterface.prompt_for_location()
        if location != None:
            datastorage.add_item(product, location)
```

Notice that we call the user interface functions to prompt the user for a product and then a location code, only proceeding if the function didn't return None. This means we only prompt for a location or add the item if the user didn't cancel.

We can now implement the equivalent function for the REMOVE action:

```
elif action == "REMOVE":
    product = userinterface.prompt_for_product()
    if product != None:
        location = userinterface.prompt_for_location()
        if location != None:
            if not datastorage.remove_item(product,
                                           location):
                pass # What to do?
```

This is almost identical to the logic for adding an item, with one exception: the datastorage.remove_item() function can fail (by returning False) if there is no inventory item for that product and location code. As the comment beside the pass statement suggests, we are going to have to do something when this happens.

We have now reached a very common point in the modular programming process: we designed all the functionality that we thought we needed, but then discovered that we missed something. When the user attempts to remove a non-existent inventory item, we will want to display an error message so the user knows what went wrong. Because all user interaction takes place within the userinterface.py module, we will want to add this functionality to that module.

Let's do that now. Go back and edit the `userinterface.py` module, and add the following function to the end:

```
def show_error(err_msg):
    print()
    print(err_msg)
    print()
```

Once again, this is an embarrassingly simple function, but it lets us keep all user interaction within the `userinterface` module (and allows for the possibility of rewriting our program later on to use a GUI). Let's now replace that `pass` statement within our `main.py` program with some appropriate error-handling code:

```
    ...
    if not datastorage.remove_item(product,
                                   location):
        userinterface.show_error(
            "There is no product with " +
            "that code at that location!")
```

Having to go back and change the functionality for a module is extremely common. Fortunately, modular programming makes this process much more self-contained, so you're less likely to get side-effects and other errors when you do this.

Now that the user can add and remove inventory items, there are just two more actions we need to implement: the INVENTORY_REPORT action, and the REORDER_REPORT action. For both of these actions, all we need to do is call the appropriate report generator function to generate the report, followed by the user interface module's `show_report()` function to display the results. Let's do this now, by adding the following code to the end of our `main()` function:

```
    elif action == "INVENTORY_REPORT":
        report = reportgenerator.generate_inventory_report()
        userinterface.show_report(report)
    elif action == "REORDER_REPORT":
        report = reportgenerator.generate_reorder_report()
        userinterface.show_report(report)
```

This completes the implementation of our `main()` function, and indeed the implementation of our entire inventory control system. Go ahead and run it. Try entering a few inventory items, removing an inventory item or two, and generating both types of report. If you have entered the code as presented in this book or downloaded the example code for this chapter, the program should work, giving you a simple but complete inventory control system—but more importantly, showing you how to implement a program using modular programming techniques.

Summary

In this chapter, we designed and implemented a non-trivial program to keep track of a company's inventory. Using the divide-and-conquer approach, we split the program into individual modules and then looked at the functionality that each module would need to provide. This led us to a more detailed design of the functions within each module, and we were then able to implement the overall system one step at a time. We discovered that some functionality had been overlooked and had to be added after the design was complete, and saw how modular programming makes it less likely for these types of changes to break your system. Finally, we had a quick play with the inventory control system to make sure it works.

In the next chapter, we will learn more about the nuts and bolts of how modules and packages work within Python.

3
Using Modules and Packages

To be able to use modules and packages within your Python programs, you need to understand how they work. In this chapter, we will examine the nuts and bolts of how modules and packages are defined and used in Python. In particular, we will:

- Review how Python modules and packages are defined
- See how packages can be created inside other packages
- Discover how modules and packages can be initialized
- Learn more about the import process
- Explore the notion of relative imports
- Learn how to control what gets imported
- Find out how to deal with circular dependencies
- See how a module can be run directly from the command line, and why this can be useful

Modules and packages

By now, you should be fairly comfortable with organizing your Python code into modules and then importing and using these modules in other modules and programs. This is only a taste of what can be done, however. Let's briefly review what Python modules and packages are before looking closer at how they work.

As we have seen, a **module** is simply a Python source file. You can import the module using the `import` statement:

```
import my_module
```

Once this is done, you can refer to any functions, classes, variables, and other definitions within the module by prepending the module name to the item, for example:

```
my_module.do_something()
print(my_module.variable)
```

In *Chapter 1*, *Introducing Modular Programming*, we learned that a Python **package** is a directory containing a special file named __init__.py. This is called the **package initialization file** and identifies the directory as a Python package. The package also typically contains one or more Python modules, for example:

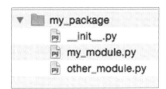

To import the modules within this package, you add the package name to the start of the module name. For example:

```
import my_package.my_module
my_package.my_module.do_something()
```

You can also use an alternative version of the import statement to make your code easier to read:

```
from my_package import my_module
my_module.do_something()
```

 We will look at the various ways in which you can use the import statement in the section *How to Import Anything* later in this chapter.

Packages within packages

Just like you can have directories within directories, you can have packages within other packages. For example, imagine that our `my_package` directory contained another directory called `my_sub_package`, which itself had an `__init__.py` file:

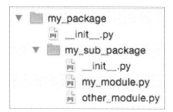

As you might expect, you import the modules within a sub-package by prepending the names of the packages that contain it:

```
from my_package.my_sub_package import my_module
my_module.do_something()
```

There is no limit to how deeply you can nest packages, though in practice it becomes a bit unwieldy if you have too many levels of packages-within-packages. More interestingly, the various packages and sub-packages form a **tree-like structure** which allows you to organize even the most complex program. For example, a sophisticated business system might be arranged like this:

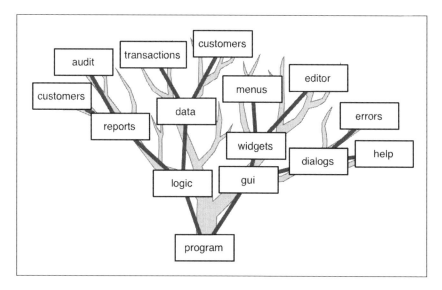

As you can see, this is called a tree-like structure because the packages-within-packages look like the spreading branches of a tree. A tree-like structure like this allows you to group logically-related parts of your program together, while ensuring that everything can be found when you need it. For example, using the structure described by the preceding illustration, you would access your customer data using the `program.logic.data.customers` package, and the various menus in your program would be defined by the `program.gui.widgets.menus` package.

Obviously, this is an extreme example. Most programs—even very complex ones—won't be this complicated. But you can see how Python packages allow you to keep your program well organized, no matter how big and elaborate it becomes.

Initializing a module

When a module is imported, any top-level code within that module is executed. This has the effect of making the various functions, variables, and classes you defined in your module available for the caller to use. To see how this works, create a new Python source file named `test_module.py`, and enter the following code into this module:

```python
def foo():
    print("in foo")

def bar():
    print("in bar")

my_var = 0

print("importing test module")
```

Now, open up a terminal window, `cd` into the directory where your `test_module.py` file is stored, and type `python` to start up the Python interpreter. Then try typing the following:

```
% import test_module
```

When you do this, the Python interpreter prints the following message:

```
importing test module
```

It does this because all the top-level Python statements in the module—including the `def` statements and our `print` statement—are executed when the module is imported. You can then call the `foo` and `bar` functions, and access the `my_var` global, by prefixing the names with `my_module`:

```
% my_module.foo()
in foo
% my_module.bar()
in bar
% print(my_module.my_var)
0
% my_module.my_var = 1
% print(my_module.my_var)
1
```

Because all the top-level Python statements are executed when a module is imported, you can initialize a module by directly including the initialization statements in the module itself, just like the statement in our test module which sets `my_var` to zero. This means that the module will be automatically initialized when the module is imported.

> Note that a module is only imported once. If two modules import the same module, the second `import` statement will simply return a reference to the already-imported module, so you won't get the same module imported (and initialized) twice.

Initialization functions

This implicit initialization works, but it isn't necessarily a good practice. One of the guidelines promoted by the designers of the Python language is that *explicit is better than implicit*. In other words, having a module automatically initialize itself isn't always good coding practice, as it isn't always clear from reading the code exactly what gets initialized and what doesn't.

To avoid this confusion, and in order to follow the Python guidelines, it is often a good idea to explicitly initialize your modules. By convention, this is done by defining a top-level function called `init()` which performs all of the initialization for your module. For example, in our `test_module`, we could replace the `my_var = 0` statement with the following:

```
def init():
    global my_var
    my_var = 0
```

This is a bit more verbose, but it makes the initialization explicit. Of course, you also have to remember to call `test_module.init()` before you use the module, usually from within your main program.

One of the main advantages of explicit module initialization is that you can control the order in which your various modules get initialized. For example, if the initialization for module A includes calling a function in module B, and this function requires module B to have been initialized, the program will crash if the two modules are imported in the wrong order. This can get particularly difficult when modules import other modules, as the order in which modules are imported can be quite confusing. To avoid this, it's better to use explicit module initialization and have your main program call `B.init()` before it calls `A.init()`. This is a perfect example of why it's generally better to use explicit initialization functions for your modules.

Initializing a package

To initialize a package, you place the Python code inside the package's `__init__.py` file. This code is then executed when the package is imported. For example, imagine that you have a package named `test_package`, which contains an `__init__.py` file and one module named `test_module.py`:

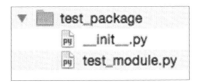

You can place whatever code you like inside the `__init__.py` file, and when the package (or a module within the package) is imported for the first time, that code will be executed.

You might be wondering why you might want to do this. Initializing a module makes sense as a module contains various functions that might need to be initialized before they are used (for example, by setting global variables to an initial value). But why initialize a package, rather than just a module within that package?

The answer lies in what happens when you import a package. When you do this, anything you define in the package's `__init__.py` file becomes available at the package level. For example, imagine that your `__init__.py` file contained the following Python code:

```
def say_hello():
    print("hello")
```

Then you could access this function from your main program in the following way:

```
import my_package
my_package.say_hello()
```

You don't need to define the `say_hello()` function inside a module within the package for it to be easily accessed.

As a general principle, however, adding code to the `__init__.py` file isn't a great idea. It works, but people looking through your package's source code will expect the package's code to be defined inside modules rather than in the package initialization file. Also, there is only one `__init__.py` file for the whole package, which makes organizing your code within the package more difficult.

A better way of using package initialization files is to write your code in modules within the package, and then use the `__init__.py` file to import this code so that it is available at the package level. For example, you might implement the `say_hello()` function within the `test_module` module, and then include the following in the package's `__init__.py` file:

```
from test_package.test_module import say_hello
```

Programs using your package would still call the `say_hello()` function in exactly the same way. The only difference is that this function is now implemented as part of the `test_module` module, rather than being lumped inside the `__init__.py` file for the entire package.

This is a very useful technique, especially as your packages get more complicated and you have lots of functions, classes, and other definitions which you want to make available. By adding `import` statements to your package initialization file, you can write the parts of your package in whatever modules make the most sense to you, and then choose which functions, classes, and so on to make available at the package level.

One of the nice things about using `__init__.py` files in this way is that the various `import` statements tell the users of your package which functions and classes they should be using; if you haven't included a module or function in your package initialization file, then it's probably excluded for a reason.

Using `import` statements in a package initialization file also tells the users of your package where the various parts of a complex package are located — the `__init__.py` file acts as a kind of index into the package's source code.

To summarize, while you can include any Python code you like within a package's `__init__.py` file, it's probably best if you limit yourself to `import` statements, and keep your real package code elsewhere.

How to import anything

So far, we have used two different versions of the `import` statement:

- Importing a module and then using the module name to access something defined within that module. For example:

```
import math
print(math.pi)
```

- Importing something from a module and then using that thing directly. For example:

```
from math import pi
print(pi)
```

The `import` statement is very powerful, however, and we can do all sorts of interesting things with it. In this section, we will look at the different ways in which you can use the `import` statement to import modules and packages, and their contents, into your program.

What does the import statement actually do?

Whenever you create a global variable or function, the Python interpreter adds the name of that variable or function to what is called the **global namespace**. The global namespace holds all the names that you have defined at the global level. To see how this works, enter the following command into the Python interpreter:

```
>>> print(globals())
```

The `globals()` built-in function returns a dictionary with the current contents of the global namespace:

```
{'__package__': None, '__doc__': None, '__name__': '__main__', '__builtins__': <module 'builtins' (built-in)>, '__loader__': <class '_frozen_importlib.BuiltinImporter'>}
```

 Don't worry about the various oddly named globals such as __package__; these are used internally by the Python interpreter.

Now, let's define a new top-level function:

```
>>> def test():
...     print("Hello")
...
>>>
```

If we now print out the dictionary of global names, our `test()` function will be included:

```
>>> print(globals())
{...'test': <function test at 0x1028225f0>...}
```

 There are several other entries in the `globals()` dictionary, but from now on we'll only show the items that interest us so that these examples aren't too confusing.

As you can see, the name `test` has been added to our global namespace.

 Once again, don't worry about the value associated with the `test` name; this is Python's internal way of storing the functions that you define.

When something is in the global namespace, you can access it by name from anywhere in your program:

```
>>> test()
Hello
```

 Note that there's a second namespace, called the **local namespace**, that holds variables and other things defined within the current function. While the local namespace is important when it comes to variable scope, we're going to ignore it as it isn't generally involved in importing modules.

Now, when you use the `import` statement, you are adding entries to the global namespace:

```
>>> import string
>>> print(globals())
{...'string': <module 'string' from '/Library/Frameworks/Python.
framework/Versions/3.3/lib/python3.3/string.py'>...}
```

As you can see, the module that you imported has been added to the global namespace, allowing you to access that module by name, for example like this:

```
>>> print(string.capwords("this is a test"))
This Is A Test
```

In the same way, if you used the from...import version of the import statement, the item you've imported will be added directly to the global namespace:

```
>>> from string import capwords
>>> print(globals())
{...'capwords': <function capwords at 0x1020fb7a0>...}
```

So now you know what the import statement does: it adds what you're importing to the global namespace so that you can access it.

Using the import statement

Now that we've seen what the import statement does, let's take a look at the different versions of the import statement that Python provides.

We've already seen the two most common forms of the import statement:

- import <something>
- from <somewhere> import <something>

With the first form, you aren't limited to importing modules one at a time. If you want, you can import multiple modules at once, like this:

```
import string, math, datetime, random
```

Similarly, you can import multiple things at once from a module or package:

```
from math import pi, radians, sin
```

If you have more items to import than will fit on one line, you can either use line continuation characters (\) to spread the import across multiple lines, or surround the list of items that you want to import with parentheses. For example:

```
from math import pi, degrees, radians, sin, cos, \
                 tan, hypot, asin, acos, atan, atan2

from math import (pi, degrees, radians, sin, cos,
                  tan, hypot, asin, acos, atan, atan2)
```

When you import something, you can also change the name of the imported item:

```
import math as math_ops
```

In this case, you are importing the math module under the name math_ops. The math module will be added to your global namespace using the name math_ops, and you can access the math module's contents using the math_ops name:

```
print(math_ops.pi)
```

There are two reasons why you might want to use the import...as statement to change the name of something when you import it:

1. To make a long or unwieldy name easier to type.

2. To avoid naming conflicts. For example, if you are using two packages that both define a module named utils, you might want to use the import...as statement so that the names are different. For example:

    ```
    from package1 import utils as utils1
    from package2 import utils as utils2
    ```

> Note that you should probably use the import...as statement sparingly. Every time you change the name of something, you (and anyone reading your code) will have to remember that X is another name for Y, which adds complexity and means that you have more things to remember as you write your program. There are certainly legitimate uses for the import...as statement, but don't overuse it.

You can, of course, combine the from...import statement with import...as:

```
from reports import customers as customer_report
from database import customers as customer_data
```

Finally, you can use a **wildcard import** to import everything from a module or package in one fell swoop:

```
from math import *
```

This adds all the items defined in the math module into the current global namespace. If you are importing from a package, then all the items defined in the package's __init__.py file will be imported.

By default, everything in the module (or package) that doesn't start with an underscore character will be imported by a wildcard import. This ensures that private variables and functions won't be imported. If you want, however, you can change what gets included in a wildcard import by using the __all__ variable; this will be discussed in the *Controlling what gets imported* section later in this chapter.

Relative imports

So far, whenever we've imported something, we've used the full name of the module or package that we want to import from. For simple imports such as `from math import pi`, this is sufficient. There are times, however, when this type of importing can be quite cumbersome.

Consider, for example, the complex tree of packages that we looked at in the *Packages within packages* section earlier in this chapter. Imagine that we want to import a module named `slider.py` from within the `program.gui.widgets.editor` package:

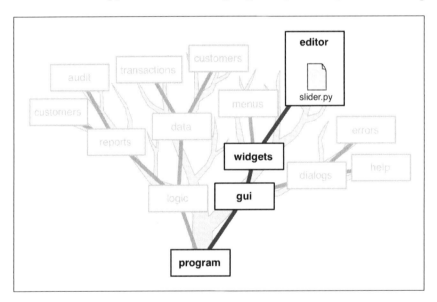

You could import this module using the following Python statement:

```
from program.gui.widgets.editor import slider
```

The `program.gui.widgets.editor` part of the `import` statement identifies the package where the `slider` module can be found.

While this works, it can be quite unwieldy, especially if you have a lot of modules to import or if one part of a package needs to import several other modules from within the same package.

To handle this type of situation, Python supports the concept of **relative imports**. Using relative imports, you identify what you want to import relative to the current module's position within the tree of packages. For example, imagine that the `slider` module wanted to import another module within the `program.gui.widgets.editor` package:

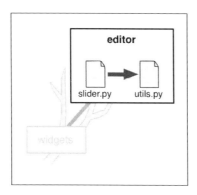

To do this, you replace the package name with a `.` character:

```
from . import slider
```

The `.` character is a shorthand for *the current package*.

In a similar way, imagine that you have a module within the `program.gui.widgets` package that wants to import the `slider` module from the `editor` sub-package:

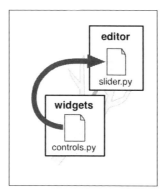

In this case, your `import` statement would look like the following:

```
from .editor import slider
```

The `.` character still refers to the current location, and `editor` is the name of the package relative to this current location. In other words, you are telling Python to look for a package named `editor` in the current location, and then import the module named `slider` within this package.

Let's consider the opposite situation. Imagine that the `slider` module wants to import a module from the `widgets` directory:

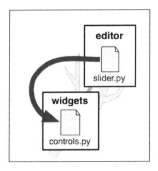

In this case, you can use two `.` characters to mean *go up one level*:

```
from .. import controls
```

As you might imagine, you can use three `.` characters to mean *go up two levels* and so on. You can also combine these techniques to move through the package hierarchy in any way you like. For example, imagine that the `slider` module wants to import a module named `errDialog` from the `gui.dialogs.errors` package:

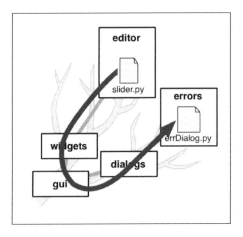

Using relative imports, the `slider` module could import the `errDialog` module in the following way:

```
from ...dialogs.errors import errDialog
```

As you can see, you can use these techniques to select any module or package anywhere in the tree of packages, relative to your current position in the tree.

There are two main reasons for using relative imports:

1. They're a great way of making your `import` statements shorter and easier to read. Instead of having to type `from program.gui.widgets.editor import utils` in the `slider` module, you can simply type `from . import utils`.

2. When you write a package for others to use, you can have different modules within your package refer to each other without having to worry about where the user installed the package. For example, I might take a package you've written and place it inside another package; using relative imports, your package will continue to work without having to change all the `import` statements to reflect the new package structure.

Like anything, relative imports can be overused. Because the meaning of the `import` statement depends on the position of the current module, relative imports tend to violate the *explicit is better than implicit* principle. You can also get into trouble if you attempt to run a module from the command line, as described in the *Running modules from the command line* section later in this chapter. For these reasons, you should use relative imports sparingly, and stick to fully listing out the entire package hierarchy in your `import` statements unless you have a good reason not to.

Controlling what gets imported

When you import a module or package, or when you use a wildcard import such as `from my_module import *`, the Python interpreter loads the contents of the given module or package into your global namespace. If you are importing from a module, all of the top-level functions, constants, classes, and other definitions will be imported. When importing from a package, all of the top-level functions, constants, and so on defined in the package's `__init__.py` file will be imported.

By default, these imports load *everything* from the given module or package. The only exception is that a wildcard import will automatically skip any function, constant, class, or other definition starting with an underscore—this has the effect of excluding private definitions from the wildcard import.

While this default behavior generally works well, there are times when you may want more control over what gets imported. To do this, you can use a special variable named __all__.

To see how the __all__ variable works, take a look at the following module:

```
A = 1
B = 2
C = 3
__all__ = ["A", "B"]
```

If you imported this module, only A and B would be imported. While the module defines the variable C, this definition would be skipped because it isn't included in the __all__ list.

Within a package, the __all__ variable behaves in the same way, with one important difference: you can also include the name of modules and sub-packages that you want to include when the package is imported. For example, a package's __init__.py file might contain only the following:

```
__all__ = ["module_1", "module_2", "sub_package"]
```

In this case, the __all__ variable controls which modules and packages to include; when you import this package, the two modules and the sub-package will be imported automatically.

Note that the preceding __init.py__ file is equivalent to the following:
```
import module1
import module2
import sub_package
```
Both versions of the __init__.py file would have the effect of including the two modules and the sub-package within the package.

While you don't need to use it, the __all__ variable gives you complete control over your imports. The __all__ variable can also be a useful way of indicating to users of your modules and packages which parts of your code they should be using: if something isn't included in the __all__ list, then it's not intended to be used by external code.

Circular dependencies

One of the annoying problems that you are likely to face while working with modules is what is known as circular dependencies. To understand what these are, consider the following two modules:

```
# module_1.py

from module_2 import calc_markup

def calc_total(items):
    total = 0
    for item in items:
        total = total + item['price']
    total = total + calc_markup(total)
    return total


# module_2.py

from module_1 import calc_total

def calc_markup(total):
    return total * 0.1

def make_sale(items):
    total_price = calc_total(items)
    ...
```

While this is a contrived example, you can see that module_1 imports something from module_2, and module_2 imports something from module_1. If you tried to run a program containing these two modules, you would see the following error when module_1 is imported:

ImportError: cannot import name calc_total

If you tried to import module_2 instead, you would get a similar error. With the code organized in this way, you're stuck: you can't import either module as both depend on the other.

To get around this, you would have to restructure your modules so that they don't depend on each other. In this example, you could create a third module, named module_3, and move the calc_markup() function to that module. This would make module_1 dependent on module_3, rather than module_2, which breaks the circular dependency.

There are other tricks you can perform to avoid circular dependency errors, for example by moving the `import` statement inside a function. In general, however, a circular dependency means that your code is badly designed, and you should refactor your code to remove the circular dependency entirely.

Running modules from the command line

In *Chapter 2, Writing Your First Modular Program*, we saw your system's main program is often named `main.py` and typically has the following structure:

```
def main():
    ...


if __name__ == "__main__":
    main()
```

The `__name__` global variable will be set to the value "`__main__`" by the Python interpreter when the user runs your program. This has the effect of calling your `main()` function when the program is run.

There is nothing special about the `main.py` program, however; it's just another Python source file. You can take advantage of this to make your Python modules executable from the command line.

Consider, for example, the following module, which we will call `double.py`:

```
def double(n):
    return n * 2


if __name__ == "__main__":
    print("double(3) =", double(3))
```

This module defines some functionality, in this case a function named `double()`, and then uses the `if __name__ == "__main__"` trick to demonstrate and test the module's functionality when it is run from the command line. Let's try running this module to see how it works:

```
% python double.py
double(3) = 6
```

Another common use for a runnable module is to allow the end user to directly access the module's functionality from the command line. To see how this works, create a new module named `funkycase.py`, and enter the following into this file:

```
def funky_case(s):
    letters = []
    capitalize = False
    for letter in s:
        if capitalize:
            letters.append(letter.upper())
        else:
            letters.append(letter.lower())
        capitalize = not capitalize
    return "".join(letters)
```

The `funky_case()` function takes a string and capitalizes every second letter. If you wanted to, you could import this module and then access this function from within your program:

```
from funkycase import funky_case
s = funky_case("Test String")
```

While this is useful, we also want to let the user run the `funkycase.py` module as a standalone program, directly converting the supplied string to funky-case and printing it out to the user can see it. To do this, we can use the `if __name__ == "__main__"` trick along with `sys.argv` to extract the string supplied by the user. We can then call the `funky_case()` function to convert this string to funky-case and print it out. To do this, add the following code to the end of your `funkycase.py` module:

```
if __name__ == "__main__":
    if len(sys.argv) != 2:
        print("You must supply exactly one string!")
    else:
        s = sys.argv[1]
        print(funky_case(s))
```

Also, add the following to the top of your module:

```
import sys
```

You can now run this module directly as if it was a standalone program:

```
% python funkycase.py "The quick brown fox"
tHe qUiCk bRoWn fOx
```

In this way, `funkycase.py` acts as a kind of *chameleon module*. To other Python source files, it appears as just another module that can be imported and used, while to the end user it looks like a standalone program that can be run from the command line.

 Note that if you want to make a module executable from the command line, you aren't limited to just using `sys.argv` to accept and process the arguments supplied by the user. The excellent `argparse` module in the Python Standard Library allows you to write Python programs (and modules) that accept a wide range of inputs and options from the user. If you haven't used this module before, do check it out.

There is one issue to be aware of when you create a module that can be run from the command line: if your module uses relative imports, your imports will fail with an *attempted relative import of non-package* error when you run it directly using the Python interpreter. This error occurs because a module forgets about its position within the package hierarchy when it is run from the command line. As long as your module doesn't use any command-line arguments, you can get around this problem by using Python's `-m` command-line option, like this:

```
python -m my_module.py
```

However, if your module does accept command-line arguments, then you will need to replace your relative imports so that this problem doesn't occur. There are workarounds, but they are kludgy and not recommended for general use.

Summary

In this chapter, we looked at the details of how Python modules and packages work. We saw that modules are simply Python source files that get imported using an `import` statement, and that packages are directories of Python source files identified by a package initialization file named __init__.py. We learned that packages can be defined inside other packages to form a tree-like structure of nested packages. We looked at how modules and packages can be initialized, and how the `import` statement can be used in various ways to import modules and packages, and their contents, into your programs.

We then saw how relative imports can be used to import modules relative to your current position in the package hierarchy and how the __all__ variable can be used to control what gets included in an import.

We then learned about circular dependencies and how to avoid them, and we finished by learning about chameleon modules, which can act as both importable modules and as standalone programs that can be run from the command line.

In the next chapter, we will apply what we have learned to the design and implementation of a more complicated program, and we will see how a good understanding of these techniques will let us build a system that is robust and can be updated to meet changing requirements.

4
Using Modules for Real-World Programming

In this chapter, we are going to use modular programming techniques to implement a useful real-world system. In particular, we will:

- Design and implement a Python package for generating charts

- See how changing requirements can be the downfall of a successful system

- Discover the ways in which modular programming techniques can help you to deal with changing requirements in the best possible way

- Learn that changing requirements can be good, because they give you the opportunity to re-think your program, resulting in more robust and well-designed code

Let's start by looking at the Python chart-generating package we are going to implement, which we will call **Charter**.

Introducing Charter

Charter will be a Python library for generating charts. Developers will be able to use Charter to convert raw numbers into good-looking line and bar charts, which can then be saved as image files. The following is an example of the sort of chart that the Charter library will be able to generate:

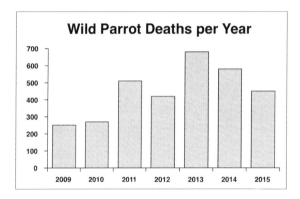

The Charter library will support line and bar charts. While we will keep Charter relatively simple by only supporting two types of charts, the package will be designed so that you can easily add more chart types and other charting options if you wish.

Designing Charter

When you look at a chart like the one shown in the previous section, you can identify a number of standard elements that are used by all types of charts. These elements include a title, the x and y axes, and one or more data series:

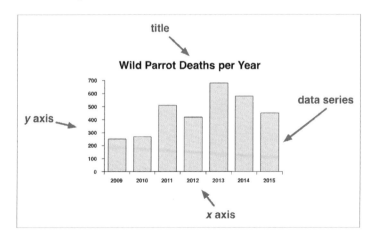

To use the Charter package, a programmer would create a new chart and set the title, the *x* and *y* axes, and the data series to be displayed. The programmer would then ask Charter to generate the chart, saving the result as an image file on disk. By combining and configuring the various elements in this way, a programmer can create any chart that they may wish to generate.

> A more sophisticated charting library would allow for additional elements, such as a *y* axis on the right-hand side, axis labels, a legend, and multiple overlapping data series. For Charter, however, we want to keep the code simple, so we will ignore these more complicated elements.

Let's take a closer look at how a programmer might interact with the Charter library, and then start to think about how it might be implemented.

We would like the programmer to be able to interact with Charter simply by importing the `charter` package and then calling various functions to work with charts. For example:

```
import charter
chart = charter.new_chart()
```

To set the title for the chart, the programmer would call the `set_title()` function:

```
charter.set_title(chart, "Wild Parrot Deaths per Year")
```

> Note that our Charter library does not use object-oriented programming techniques. Using object-oriented techniques, the chart title would be set using a statement such as `chart.set_title("Wild Parrot Deaths per Year")`. However, object-oriented techniques are beyond the scope of this book, and so we will use a simpler procedural programming style for the Charter library.

To set the *x* and *y* axes for a chart, the programmer would have to supply enough information so that Charter can generate the chart and display these axes. To understand how this might work, let's think about what an axis looks like.

For some charts, an axis might represent a range of values:

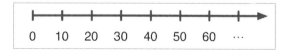

In this case, a data point would be displayed by calculating the position of the point along the axis. For example, a data point with $x = 35$ would be displayed halfway between the **30** and **40** points on this axis.

We are going to call this type of axis a **continuous axis**. Notice how, for this type of axis, the labels are positioned below the tick marks. Compare this with the following axis, which is divided up into a number of discrete "buckets":

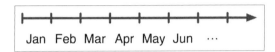

In this case, each data point corresponds to a single bucket, and the label would appear in the space between the tick marks. This type of axis will be called a **discrete axis**.

Notice that for continuous axes, the labels are displayed on the tick marks, while for discrete axes the labels are displayed between the tick marks. Also, the values for a discrete axis can be anything (in this case, month names), while for continuous axes, the values must be numbers.

For the Charter library, we are going to make the x axis a discrete axis, while the y axis will be continuous. In theory, you could use either type of axis for both the x and y axes, but we are keeping this simple to make the library easier to implement.

Knowing this, we can now look at how the various axes can be defined when creating a chart.

To define the x axis, the programmer will call the `set_x_axis()` function with a list of labels to use for each bucket within the discrete axis:

```
charter.set_x_axis(chart,
                   ["2009", "2010", "2011", "2012", "2013",
                   "2014", "2015"])
```

Each entry in the list corresponds to a single bucket within the axis.

For the y axis, we need to define both the range of values that will be displayed and how these will be labeled. To do this, we're going to need to supply minimum, maximum, and label values to the `set_y_axis()` function:

```
charter.set_y_axis(chart, minimum=0, maximum=700,
              labels=[0, 100, 200, 300, 400, 500, 600, 700])
```

To keep things simple, we will assume that the *y* axis uses a linear scale. We could potentially support other types of scaling, for example to implement a logarithmic axis, but we're going to ignore this as it would make the Charter library more complicated.

Now that we know how the axes will be defined, we can look at how the data series will be specified. Firstly, we need the programmer to tell Charter what type of data series to display:

```
charter.set_series_type(chart, "bar")
```

As mentioned earlier, we will support both line and bar charts.

The programmer then needs to specify the contents of the data series. Since our *x* axis is discrete while the *y* axis is continuous, we can define a data series as a list of *y* axis values, one for each discrete *x* axis value:

```
charter.set_series(chart, [250, 270, 510, 420, 680, 580, 450])
```

This completes the definition of a chart. Once it has been defined, the programmer can ask the Charter library to generate the chart:

```
charter.generate_chart(chart, "chart.png")
```

Putting all this together, here is a complete program that generates the bar chart shown at the start of this chapter:

```
import charter
chart = charter.new_chart()
charter.set_title(chart, "Wild Parrot Deaths per Year")
charter.set_x_axis(chart,
                    ["2009", "2010", "2011", "2012", "2013",
                     "2014", "2015"])
charter.set_y_axis(chart, minimum=0, maximum=700,
                    labels=[0, 100, 200, 300, 400, 500, 600, 700])
charter.set_series(chart, [250, 270, 510, 420, 680, 580, 450])
charter.set_series_type(chart, "bar")
charter.generate_chart(chart, "chart.png")
```

Because Charter is a library intended to be used by programmers, this code gives a fairly complete specification for the Charter library's API. It's clear from this example program what is supposed to happen. Let's now look at how this can be implemented.

Implementing Charter

We know that the Charter library's public interface will consist of a number of functions accessed at the package level, for example `charter.new_chart()`. However, using the techniques covered in the previous chapter, we know that we don't have to define our library's API in the package initialization file to make these functions available at the package level. Instead, we can define the functions elsewhere, and import them into the `__init__.py` file so that they are available for others to use.

Let's start by creating a directory to hold our `charter` package. Create a new directory named `charter`, and create within it an empty package initialization file, `__init__.py`. This gives us the basic framework within which to write our library:

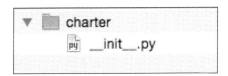

Based on our design, we know that the process of generating a chart will involve the following three steps:

1. Create a new chart by calling the `new_chart()` function.

2. Define the contents and appearance of the chart by calling the various `set_XXX()` functions.

3. Generate the chart and save it as an image file by calling the `generate_chart()` function.

To keep our code nicely organized, we're going to separate the process of generating a chart from the process of creating and defining a chart. To do this, we'll have a module named `chart`, which handles the chart creation and definition, and a separate module named `generator` which handles the chart generation.

Go ahead and create these two new empty modules, placing them inside the `charter` package:

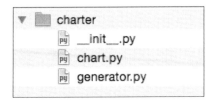

Now that we have an overall structure for our package, let's create some placeholders for the various functions that we know we're going to have to implement. Edit the `chart.py` module, and enter the following into this file:

```
def new_chart():
    pass

def set_title(chart, title):
    pass

def set_x_axis(chart, x_axis):
    pass

def set_y_axis(chart, minimum, maximum, labels):
    pass

def set_series_type(chart, series_type):
    pass

def set_series(chart, series):
    pass
```

Similarly, edit the `generator.py` module, and enter the following into it:

```
def generate_chart(chart, filename):
    pass
```

These are all the functions that we know we'll need to implement for the Charter library. However, they're not in the correct place yet—we want the user to be able to call `charter.new_chart()`, not `charter.chart.new_chart()`. To get around this, edit the `__init__.py` file, and enter the following into this file:

```
from .chart     import *
from .generator import *
```

As you can see, we're using relative imports to load all the functions from these modules into the main `charter` package's namespace.

Our Charter library is starting to take shape! Let's now work on each of the two modules in turn.

Implementing the chart.py module

Since we're eschewing the use of object-oriented programming techniques in our implementation of the Charter library, we can't use an object to store the information about a chart. Instead, the `new_chart()` function is going to return a chart value, and the various `set_XXX()` functions will take that chart and add information to it.

The easiest way to store information about a chart is to use a Python dictionary. This makes the implementation of our `new_chart()` function very simple; edit the `chart.py` module and replace the placeholder for `new_chart()` with the following:

```
def new_chart():
    return {}
```

Once we have a dictionary that will hold the chart's data, it's easy to store the various values we want into this dictionary. For example, edit the definition for the `set_title()` function so that it looks like the following:

```
def set_title(chart, title):
    chart['title'] = title
```

In a similar way, we can implement the rest of the `set_XXX()` functions:

```
def set_x_axis(chart, x_axis):
    chart['x_axis'] = x_axis

def set_y_axis(chart, minimum, maximum, labels):
    chart['y_min']    = minimum
    chart['y_max']    = maximum
    chart['y_labels'] = labels

def set_series_type(chart, series_type):
    chart['series_type'] = series_type

def set_series(chart, series):
    chart['series'] = series
```

This completes the implementation for our `chart.py` module.

Implementing the generator.py module

Unfortunately, the `generate_chart()` function is going to be more difficult to implement, which is why we moved this function into a separate module. The process of generating a chart will involve the following steps:

1. Create an empty image to hold the generated chart.

2. Draw the chart's title.

3. Draw the *x* axis.

4. Draw the *y* axis.

5. Draw the data series.

6. Save the resulting image file to disk.

Because the process of generating a chart requires us to work with images, we're going to need to find a library that allows us to generate image files. Let's grab one now.

The Pillow library

The **Python Imaging Library (PIL)** is a venerable library used to generate images. Unfortunately, PIL is no longer being actively developed. There is, however, a newer version of PIL, named **Pillow**, that continues to be supported and will allow us to create and save image files.

The main web site for the Pillow library can be found at `http://python-pillow.org/`, and the documentation is available at `http://pillow.readthedocs.org/`.

Let's go ahead and install Pillow. The easiest way to do this is to use `pip install pillow`, although the installation guide (`http://pillow.readthedocs.org/en/3.0.x/installation.html`) gives you a variety of options if this won't work for you.

Looking through the Pillow documentation, it appears that we can create an empty image using the following code:

```
from PIL import Image
image = Image.new("RGB", (CHART_WIDTH, CHART_HEIGHT), "#7f00ff")
```

This creates a new RGB (red, green, blue) image with the given width and height, filled with the given color.

#7f00ff is a hexadecimal color code for purple. Each pair of hexadecimal digits represents a color value: 7f for red, 00 for green, and ff for blue.

To draw into this image, we will use the `ImageDraw` module. For example:

```
from PIL import ImageDraw
drawer = ImageDraw.Draw(image)
drawer.line(50, 50, 150, 200, fill="#ff8010", width=2)
```

Once the chart has been drawn, we can save the image to disk in the following way:

```
image.save("image.png", format="png")
```

This brief introduction to the Pillow library tells us how to implement steps 1 and 6 of the chart-generation process we described earlier. It also tells us that for steps 2 to 5, we are going to use the `ImageDraw` module to draw the various chart elements.

Renderers

When we draw the chart, we want to be able to choose the elements to draw. For example, we might select between the `"bar"` and `"line"` elements depending on the type of data series the user wants to display. A very simple way of doing this would be to structure our drawing code like this:

```
if chart['series_type'] == "bar":
    ...draw the data series using bars
elif chart['series_type'] == "line":
    ...draw the data series using lines
```

However, this isn't very expandable and would quickly get hard to read if the drawing logic gets complicated, or if we added more charting options to the library. To make the Charter library more modular, and to support enhancing it down the track, we will make use of renderer modules to do the actual drawing for us.

In computer graphics, a **renderer** is a part of a program that draws something. The idea is that you can select the appropriate renderer and ask it to draw the element you want without having to worry about the details of how that element will be drawn.

Using renderer modules, our drawing logic would look something like the following:

```
from renderers import bar_series, line_series

if chart['series_type'] == "bar":
    bar_series.draw(chart, drawer)
elif chart['series_type'] == "line":
    line_series.draw(chart, drawer)
```

This means that we can leave the actual details of how each element is drawn to the renderer module itself and not clutter up our `generate_chart()` function with lots of detailed drawing code.

To keep track of our renderer modules, we're going to create a sub-package named `renderers`, and place all our renderer modules inside this sub-package. Let's create this sub-package now.

Create a new directory named `renderers` within the main `charter` directory, and create a new file inside it called `__init__.py` to act as the package initialization file. This file can be empty as we don't need to do anything special to initialize this sub-package.

We are going to need a total of five different renderer modules for the Charter library:

- `title.py`
- `x_axis.py`
- `y_axis.py`
- `bar_series.py`
- `line_series.py`

Go ahead and create these five files within the `charter.renderers` directory, and enter the following placeholder text into each one:

```
def draw(chart, drawer):
    pass
```

This gives us the overall structure for our renderer modules. Let's now use these renderers to implement our `generate_chart()` function.

Edit the `generate.py` module, and replace the placeholder definition for the `generate_chart()` function with the following:

```
def generate_chart(chart, filename):
    image   = Image.new("RGB", (CHART_WIDTH, CHART_HEIGHT),
                        "#ffffff")
```

```
drawer = ImageDraw.Draw(image)

title.draw(chart, drawer)
x_axis.draw(chart, drawer)
y_axis.draw(chart, drawer)
if chart['series_type'] == "bar":
    bar_series.draw(chart, drawer)
elif chart['series_type'] == "line":
    line_series.draw(chart, drawer)

image.save(filename, format="png")
```

As you can see, we create an `Image` object to hold our generated chart, initializing it to white using the hex color code `#ffffff`. We then use the `ImageDraw` module to define a `drawer` object to draw into the chart and call the various renderer modules to do all the work. Finally, we call `image.save()` to save the image file to disk.

For this function to work, we need to add a few `import` statements to the top of our `generator.py` module:

```
from PIL import Image, ImageDraw
from .renderers import (title, x_axis, y_axis,
                        bar_series, line_series)
```

There's one more thing that we haven't dealt with yet: when we create the image, we make use of two constants which tell Pillow the dimensions of the image to create:

```
image = Image.new("RGB", (CHART_WIDTH, CHART_HEIGHT),
                  "#ffffff")
```

We need to define these two constants somewhere.

As it turns out, we are going to need to define several more constants and use them throughout the Charter library. To allow for this, we'll create a special module just to hold our various constants.

Create a new file named `constants.py` within the top-level `charter` directory. Inside this module, add the following values:

```
CHART_WIDTH  = 600
CHART_HEIGHT = 400
```

Then, add the following `import` statement to your `generator.py` module:

```
from .constants import *
```

Testing the code

While we haven't implemented any of our renderers, we have enough code in place to start testing. To do this, create an empty file named `test_charter.py`, and place it in the directory containing the `charter` package. Then, enter the following into this file:

```
import charter
chart = charter.new_chart()
charter.set_title(chart, "Wild Parrot Deaths per Year")
charter.set_x_axis(chart,
                   ["2009", "2010", "2011", "2012", "2013",
                    "2014", "2015"])
charter.set_y_axis(chart, minimum=0, maximum=700,
                   labels=[0, 100, 200, 300, 400, 500, 600, 700])
charter.set_series(chart, [250, 270, 510, 420, 680, 580, 450])
charter.set_series_type(chart, "bar")
charter.generate_chart(chart, "chart.png")
```

This is just a copy of the example code we saw earlier. This script will allow you to test the Charter library; open up a terminal or command-line window, `cd` into the directory containing the `test_charter.py` file, and type the following:

python test_charter.py

All going well, the program should finish without any errors. You can then look at the `chart.png` file, which should be an empty image file filled with a white background.

Rendering the title

We next need to implement our various renderer modules, starting with the chart's title. Edit the `renderers/title.py` file, and replace your placeholder definition of the `draw()` function with the following:

```
def draw(chart, drawer):
    font = ImageFont.truetype("Helvetica", 24)
    text_width,text_height = font.getsize(chart['title'])

    left = CHART_WIDTH/2 - text_width/2
    top  = TITLE_HEIGHT/2 - text_height/2

    drawer.text((left, top), chart['title'], "#4040a0", font)
```

This renderer starts by obtaining a font to use when drawing the title. It then calculates the size (in pixels) of the title text and the position to use for the label so that it is nicely centered on the chart. Notice that we use a constant named TITLE_HEIGHT to specify the amount of space to use for the chart's title.

The final line in this function draws the title onto the chart using the specified position and font. The string #4040a0 is the hexadecimal color code to use for the text—this is a dark blue color.

Because this module uses the ImageFont module to load the font, as well as some constants from our constants.py module, we need to add the following import statements to the top of our module:

```
from PIL import ImageFont
from ..constants import *
```

Note that we use .. to import the constants module from our parent package.

Finally, we need to add the TITLE_HEIGHT constant to our constants.py module:

```
TITLE_HEIGHT = 50
```

If you now run your test_charter.py script, you should see the chart's title appear in the generated image:

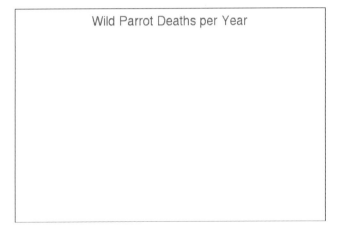

Rendering the x axis

If you remember, the *x* axis is a discrete axis with labels displayed between each tick mark. To draw this, we are going to have to calculate the width of each "bucket" on the axis, and then draw lines to represent the axis and the tick marks, as well as drawing the label for each bucket.

Start by editing the `renderers/x_axis.py` file, and replace your placeholder `draw()` function with the following:

```python
def draw(chart, drawer):
    font = ImageFont.truetype("Helvetica", 12)
    label_height = font.getsize("Test")[1]

    avail_width = CHART_WIDTH - Y_AXIS_WIDTH - MARGIN
    bucket_width = avail_width / len(chart['x_axis'])

    axis_top = CHART_HEIGHT - X_AXIS_HEIGHT
    drawer.line([(Y_AXIS_WIDTH, axis_top),
                 (CHART_WIDTH - MARGIN, axis_top)],
                "#4040a0", 2) # Draw main axis line.

    left = Y_AXIS_WIDTH
    for bucket_num in range(len(chart['x_axis'])):
        drawer.line([(left, axis_top),
                     (left, axis_top + TICKMARK_HEIGHT)],
                    "#4040a0", 1) # Draw tickmark.

        label_width = font.getsize(chart['x_axis'][bucket_num])[0]
        label_left = max(left,
                         left + bucket_width/2 - label_width/2)
        label_top  = axis_top + TICKMARK_HEIGHT + 4

        drawer.text((label_left, label_top),
                    chart['x_axis'][bucket_num], "#000000", font)

        left = left + bucket_width

    drawer.line([(left, axis_top),
                 (left, axis_top + TICKMARK_HEIGHT)],
                "#4040a0", 1) # Draw final tickmark.
```

You'll also need to add the following `import` statements at the top of your module:

```python
from PIL import ImageFont
from ..constants import *
```

Finally, you should add the following definitions to your `constants.py` module:

```python
X_AXIS_HEIGHT    = 50
Y_AXIS_WIDTH     = 50
MARGIN           = 20
TICKMARK_HEIGHT  = 8
```

These define the sizes of the fixed elements within the chart.

If you now run your `test_charter.py` script, you should see the *x* axis displayed along the bottom of the chart:

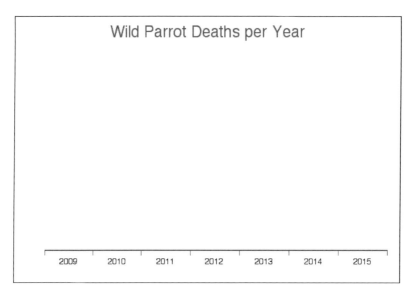

The remaining renderers

As you can see, the generated image is starting to look more chart-like. Since the purpose of this package is to show how to structure your code, rather than the details of how these modules are implemented, let's skip ahead and add the remaining renderers without further discussion.

Start by editing your `renderers/y_axis.py` file to look like the following:

```python
from PIL import ImageFont

from ..constants import *

def draw(chart, drawer):
    font = ImageFont.truetype("Helvetica", 12)
    label_height = font.getsize("Test")[1]

    axis_top    = TITLE_HEIGHT
    axis_bottom = CHART_HEIGHT - X_AXIS_HEIGHT
    axis_height = axis_bottom - axis_top
```

```
drawer.line([(Y_AXIS_WIDTH, axis_top),
             (Y_AXIS_WIDTH, axis_bottom)],
            "#4040a0", 2) # Draw main axis line.

for y_value in chart['y_labels']:
    y = ((y_value - chart['y_min']) /
         (chart['y_max']-chart['y_min']))

    y_pos = axis_top + (axis_height - int(y * axis_height))

    drawer.line([(Y_AXIS_WIDTH - TICKMARK_HEIGHT, y_pos),
                 (Y_AXIS_WIDTH, y_pos)],
                "#4040a0", 1) # Draw tickmark.

    label_width,label_height = font.getsize(str(y_value))
    label_left = Y_AXIS_WIDTH-TICKMARK_HEIGHT-label_width-4
    label_top = y_pos - label_height / 2

    drawer.text((label_left, label_top), str(y_value),
                "#000000", font)
```

Next, edit renderers/bar_series.py to look like this:

```
from PIL import ImageFont
from ..constants import *

def draw(chart, drawer):
    avail_width  = CHART_WIDTH - Y_AXIS_WIDTH - MARGIN
    bucket_width = avail_width / len(chart['x_axis'])

    max_top      = TITLE_HEIGHT
    bottom       = CHART_HEIGHT - X_AXIS_HEIGHT
    avail_height = bottom - max_top

    left = Y_AXIS_WIDTH
    for y_value in chart['series']:

        bar_left = left + MARGIN / 2
        bar_right = left + bucket_width - MARGIN / 2

        y = ((y_value - chart['y_min']) /
             (chart['y_max'] - chart['y_min']))

        bar_top = max_top + (avail_height - int(y * avail_height))
```

```
drawer.rectangle([(bar_left, bar_top),
                  (bar_right + 1,
                   bottom)],
                 fill="#e8e8f4", outline="#4040a0")

        left = left + bucket_width
```

Finally, edit `renderers.line_series.py` to look like the following:

```python
from PIL import ImageFont
from ..constants import *

def draw(chart, drawer):
    avail_width  = CHART_WIDTH - Y_AXIS_WIDTH - MARGIN
    bucket_width = avail_width / len(chart['x_axis'])

    max_top      = TITLE_HEIGHT
    bottom       = CHART_HEIGHT - X_AXIS_HEIGHT
    avail_height = bottom - max_top

    left   = Y_AXIS_WIDTH
    prev_y = None
    for y_value in chart['series']:
        y = ((y_value - chart['y_min']) /
             (chart['y_max'] - chart['y_min']))

        cur_y = max_top + (avail_height - int(y * avail_height))

        if prev_y != None:
            drawer.line([(left - bucket_width / 2, prev_y),
                         (left + bucket_width / 2), cur_y],
                        fill="#4040a0", width=1)
        prev_y = cur_y
        left = left + bucket_width
```

This completes our implementation of the Charter library.

Testing Charter

If you run the `test_charter.py` script, you should see a complete bar chart:

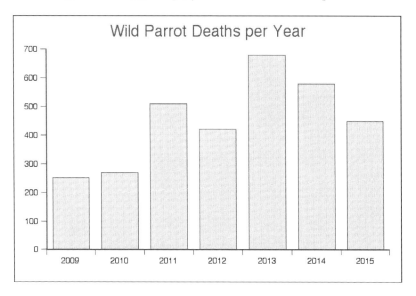

There is obviously a lot more that we could do with the Charter library, but even in its current state, it works well. If you want, you can use it to generate line and bar charts for all sorts of data. For our purposes, we can declare the Charter library to be complete, and start using it as part of our production system.

The fly in the ointment – changing requirements

Of course, nothing is ever really finished. Let's pretend that you wrote the Charter library and have been busily extending it for several months, adding more data series types and lots of options. The library is being used in several big projects for your company, the output looks fantastic, and everyone seems to be very happy with it—until the day that your boss comes in and says, "It's too fuzzy. Can you take the fuzziness away?"

You ask what he means, and he says that he's been printing the charts out on a high-resolution laser printer. The results aren't good enough for him to use in his company reports. He takes a printout and points to the heading. Looking closely, you can see what he means:

Sure enough, the text is pixelated, and even the lines look a bit jagged when printed at high resolution. You try increasing the size of the generated chart, but it still doesn't look good enough—and when you try increasing the size to match the 1,200 dots per inch of the company's high-resolution laser printer, your program crashes.

"But the program was never designed for that," you complain. "We wrote it to show charts on-screen."

"I don't care," says your boss. "I want you to generate the output in vector format. That always prints fine, and isn't fuzzy at all."

> Just in case you haven't encountered this before, there are two fundamentally different ways of storing image data: bitmapped images, which are made up of pixels, and vector images, where the individual drawing instructions (for example, "write some text", "draw a line," "fill a rectangle," and so on) are saved, and then these instructions are followed each time the image is to be displayed. Bitmapped images suffer from pixelation or "fuzziness," while vector images look great even when enlarged or printed at a high resolution.

You do a quick Google search, and confirm that the Pillow library can't save vector-format images; it only works with bitmapped data. Your boss isn't sympathetic, "Just make it work in vector format, saving to PDF as well as PNG for those people already using it."

With a sinking heart, you wonder how you could possibly meet these new requirements. The whole Charter library has been built from the ground up to generate bitmapped PNG images. Won't you have to rewrite the whole thing from scratch?

Redesigning Charter

As the Charter library now needs to optionally save the chart as a vector-format PDF file, we need to find an alternative to the Python Imaging Library that supports writing to PDF files. There is one obvious candidate for this: **ReportLab**.

ReportLab is a commercial PDF generator, which is also released under an open source license. You can find out more about the ReportLab toolkit at `http://www.reportlab.com/opensource/`. The easiest way to install ReportLab is to use `pip install reportlab`. If this doesn't work for you, check out the installation instructions at `https://bitbucket.org/rptlab/reportlab` for more details. Documentation for the ReportLab toolkit can be found at `http://www.reportlab.com/docs/reportlab-userguide.pdf`.

In many ways, ReportLab works in the same way as the Python Imaging Library: you initialize a document (called a **canvas** in ReportLab), call various methods to draw the elements onto the canvas, and then use the `save()` method to save the PDF file to disk.

There is one additional step, however: because the PDF file format supports multiple pages, you need to call the `showPage()` function to render the current page before saving the document. While we don't need multiple pages for the Charter library, we could create multi-page PDF documents by calling `showPage()` after drawing each page, and then call `save()` to save the file to disk when we are finished.

Now that we have a tool that allows us to generate PDF files, let's take a look at how we can restructure the Charter package to support rendering in either PNG or PDF file format.

The `generate_chart()` function seems to be the logical point at which the user should be able to choose the output format. In fact, we can detect the format automatically based on the file name—if the `filename` parameter ends with `.pdf`, then we should generate the chart in PDF format, while if the `filename` ends with `.png`, then we should generate the file in PNG format.

More generally, though, we have a problem with our renderers: they're all designed to work with the Python Imaging Library, and use the `ImageDraw` module to draw each chart as a bitmapped image.

Because of this, and the complexity of the code inside each renderer module, it makes sense to leave these renderers alone and write new renderers that use ReportLab to generate the chart's elements in PDF format. To do this, we are going to need to **refactor** our rendering code.

Before we leap in and start making changes, let's think about what we want to achieve. We'll need to have two separate versions of each renderer — one to generate the element in PNG format and the other to generate the same element in PDF format:

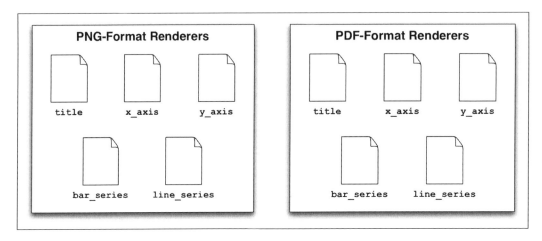

Since all of these modules do the same thing — draw an element onto the chart — it would be good to have a single function that calls the appropriate renderer module's `draw()` function to draw a given chart element in the desired output format. This way, the rest of our code will only need to call one function, rather than choose between ten different `draw()` functions depending on the desired element and format.

To do this, we'll add a new module called `renderer.py` within the `renderers` package, and leave calling the individual renderers to that module. This will simplify our design immensely.

Finally, our `generate_chart()` function is going to have to create a ReportLab canvas to generate the chart in PDF format, and then save this canvas when the chart has been generated, just like it does at the moment for the bitmapped image.

All this means that, while we have some work to do implementing new versions of our renderer modules, creating a new `renderer.py` module and updating the `generate_chart()` function, the rest of the system will remain exactly the same. We don't need to rewrite everything from scratch, and the rest of our modules — in particular, the existing renderers — don't have to be changed at all. Whew!

Refactoring the code

We'll start our refactoring by moving the existing PNG renderers into a new sub-package called `renderers.png`. Create a new directory named `png` within the `renderers` directory, and move the `title.py`, `x_axis.py`, `y_axis.py`, `bar_series.py` and `line_series.py` modules into this directory. Then, create an empty package initialization file, `__init__.py`, inside the `png` directory so that Python will recognize it as a package.

There is one minor change we are going to have to make to our existing PNG renderers: because each renderer module imports the `constants.py` module using a relative import, we will need to update these modules so that they can still find the `constants` module from their new position. To do this, edit each PNG renderer module in turn, and find the line that looks like the following:

```
from ..constants import *
```

Add an extra `.` to each of these lines so that they look like this:

```
from ...constants import *
```

Our next task is to create a package to hold our PDF-format renderers. Create a sub-directory named `pdf` in the `renderers` directory, and create an empty package initialization file in that directory to make it a Python package.

We next want to implement the `renderer.py` module we talked about earlier so that our `generate_chart()` function can concentrate on drawing chart elements rather than worrying about which module each element is defined in. Create a new file named `renderer.py` inside the `renderers` directory, and add the following code to this file:

```
from .png import title       as title_png
from .png import x_axis      as x_axis_png
from .png import y_axis      as y_axis_png
from .png import bar_series  as bar_series_png
from .png import line_series as line_series_png

renderers = {
    'png' : {
        'title'       : title_png,
        'x_axis'      : x_axis_png,
        'y_axis'      : y_axis_png,
        'bar_series'  : bar_series_png,
        'line_series' : line_series_png
    },
}

def draw(format, element, chart, output):
    renderers[format][element].draw(chart, output)
```

This module is doing something tricky, which you may not have encountered before: after importing each PNG-format renderer module using `import...as`, we then treat the imported modules as if they were Python variables, storing a reference to each module in the `renderers` dictionary. Our `draw()` function then selects the appropriate module from that dictionary using `renderers[format][element]`, and calls the `draw()` function within that module to do the actual drawing.

This Python trick saves us a lot of coding—without it, we would have had to write a whole series of `if...then` statements to call the appropriate module's `draw()` function based on the desired element and format. Using a dictionary in this way saves us a lot of typing and makes the code much easier to read and debug.

> We could have also used the Python Standard Library's `importlib` module to load a renderer module by name. This would have made our `renderer` module even shorter but would have made it harder to understand the code. Using `import...as` and a dictionary to select the desired module is a good trade-off between complexity and comprehensibility.

We next need to update our `generate_report()` function. As discussed in the previous section, we want to choose the output format based on the file extension for the file being generated. We also need to update this function to use our new `renderer.draw()` function, rather than importing and calling the renderer modules directly.

Edit the `generator.py` module, and replace the contents of this module with the following code:

```python
from PIL import Image, ImageDraw
from reportlab.pdfgen.canvas import Canvas

from .constants import *
from .renderers import renderer

def generate_chart(chart, filename):

    # Select the output format.

    if filename.lower().endswith(".pdf"):
        format = "pdf"
    elif filename.lower().endswith(".png"):
        format = "png"
    else:
        print("Unsupported file format: " + filename)
```

```
        return

    # Prepare the output file based on the file format.

    if format == "pdf":
        output = Canvas(filename)
    elif format == "png":
        image  = Image.new("RGB", (CHART_WIDTH, CHART_HEIGHT),
                           "#ffffff")
        output = ImageDraw.Draw(image)

    # Draw the various chart elements.

    renderer.draw(format, "title",  chart, output)
    renderer.draw(format, "x_axis", chart, output)
    renderer.draw(format, "y_axis", chart, output)
    if chart['series_type'] == "bar":
        renderer.draw(format, "bar_series", chart, output)
    elif chart['series_type'] == "line":
        renderer.draw(format, "line_series", chart, output)

    # Finally, save the output to disk.

    if format == "pdf":
        output.showPage()
        output.save()
    elif format == "png":
        image.save(filename, format="png")
```

There's a lot of code in this module, but the comments should help to explain what is going on. As you can see, we use the supplied file name to set the format variable to "pdf" or "png" as appropriate. We then prepare the output variable to hold the generated image or PDF file. Next, we call renderer.draw() to draw each chart element in turn, passing in the format and output variables so that the renderer can do its job. Finally, we save the output to disk so that the chart will be saved to the appropriate PDF or PNG format file.

With these changes in place, you should be able to use the updated Charter package to generate a PNG-format file. PDF files won't work yet because we haven't written the PDF renderers, but PNG format output should be working. Go ahead and test this by running the test_charter.py script, just to make sure you haven't made any typos entering the code.

Now that we've finished refactoring our existing code, let's add our PDF renderers.

Implementing the PDF renderer modules

We will work through the various renderer modules one at a time. Start by creating the `titles.py` module inside the `pdf` directory, and enter the following code into this file:

```python
from ...constants import *

def draw(chart, canvas):
    text_width  = canvas.stringWidth(chart['title'],
                                     "Helvetica", 24)
    text_height = 24 * 1.2

    left   = CHART_WIDTH/2 - text_width/2
    bottom = CHART_HEIGHT - TITLE_HEIGHT/2 + text_height/2

    canvas.setFont("Helvetica", 24)
    canvas.setFillColorRGB(0.25, 0.25, 0.625)
    canvas.drawString(left, bottom, chart['title'])
```

In some ways, this code is quite similar to the PNG version of this renderer: we calculate the width and height of the text and use this to calculate the position on the chart where the title should be drawn. We then draw the title in 24-point Helvetica font, in a dark blue color.

There are, however, some important differences:

- The way we calculate the width and the height of the text is different. For the width, we call the canvas's `stringWidth()` function, while for the height, we multiply the font size of the text by 1.2. By default, ReportLab leaves a gap of 20% of the font size between lines of text, so multiplying the font size by 1.2 is an accurate way of calculating the height of a line of text.

- The units used to calculate the position of elements on the page are different. ReportLab measures all positions and sizes using **points** rather than pixels. A point is roughly 1/72nd of an inch. Fortunately, one point is fairly close to the size of a pixel on a typical computer screen; this allows us to ignore the different measurement systems and have the PDF output still look good.

- PDF files use a different coordinate system to PNG files. In a PNG-format file, the top of the image has a *y* value of zero, while for PDF files *y=0* is at the bottom of the image. This means that all our positions on the page have to be calculated relative to the bottom of the page, rather than the top of the image as was done with the PNG renderers.

- The colors are specified using RGB color values, where each component of the color is given as a number between zero and one. For example, a color value of (0.25,0.25,0.625) is equivalent to the hex color code #4040a0.

Without further ado, let's implement the remaining PDF renderer modules. The x_axis.py module should look like the following:

```
def draw(chart, canvas):
    label_height = 12 * 1.2

    avail_width  = CHART_WIDTH - Y_AXIS_WIDTH - MARGIN
    bucket_width = avail_width / len(chart['x_axis'])

    axis_top = X_AXIS_HEIGHT
    canvas.setStrokeColorRGB(0.25, 0.25, 0.625)
    canvas.setLineWidth(2)
    canvas.line(Y_AXIS_WIDTH, axis_top,
                CHART_WIDTH - MARGIN, axis_top)

    left = Y_AXIS_WIDTH
    for bucket_num in range(len(chart['x_axis'])):
        canvas.setLineWidth(1)
        canvas.line(left, axis_top,
                    left, axis_top - TICKMARK_HEIGHT)

        label_width  = canvas.stringWidth(
                            chart['x_axis'][bucket_num],
                            "Helvetica", 12)
        label_left   = max(left,
                           left + bucket_width/2 - label_width/2)
        label_bottom = axis_top - TICKMARK_HEIGHT-4-label_height

        canvas.setFont("Helvetica", 12)
        canvas.setFillColorRGB(0.0, 0.0, 0.0)
        canvas.drawString(label_left, label_bottom,
                          chart['x_axis'][bucket_num])

        left = left + bucket_width

    canvas.setStrokeColorRGB(0.25, 0.25, 0.625)
    canvas.setLineWidth(1)
    canvas.line(left, axis_top, left, axis_top - TICKMARK_HEIGHT)
```

Similarly, the `y_axis.py` module should be implemented as follows:

```
from ...constants import *

def draw(chart, canvas):
    label_height = 12 * 1.2

    axis_top    = CHART_HEIGHT - TITLE_HEIGHT
    axis_bottom = X_AXIS_HEIGHT
    axis_height = axis_top - axis_bottom

    canvas.setStrokeColorRGB(0.25, 0.25, 0.625)
    canvas.setLineWidth(2)
    canvas.line(Y_AXIS_WIDTH, axis_top, Y_AXIS_WIDTH, axis_bottom)

    for y_value in chart['y_labels']:
        y = ((y_value - chart['y_min']) /
             (chart['y_max'] - chart['y_min']))

        y_pos = axis_bottom + int(y * axis_height)

        canvas.setLineWidth(1)
        canvas.line(Y_AXIS_WIDTH - TICKMARK_HEIGHT, y_pos,
                    Y_AXIS_WIDTH, y_pos)

        label_width = canvas.stringWidth(str(y_value),
                                         "Helvetica", 12)
        label_left  = Y_AXIS_WIDTH - TICKMARK_HEIGHT-label_width-4
        label_bottom = y_pos - label_height/4

        canvas.setFont("Helvetica", 12)
        canvas.setFillColorRGB(0.0, 0.0, 0.0)
        canvas.drawString(label_left, label_bottom, str(y_value))
```

For the `bar_series.py` module, enter the following:

```
from ...constants import *

def draw(chart, canvas):
    avail_width  = CHART_WIDTH - Y_AXIS_WIDTH - MARGIN
    bucket_width = avail_width / len(chart['x_axis'])

    bottom       = X_AXIS_HEIGHT
    max_top      = CHART_HEIGHT - TITLE_HEIGHT
```

```
    avail_height = max_top - bottom

    left = Y_AXIS_WIDTH
    for y_value in chart['series']:
        bar_left  = left + MARGIN / 2
        bar_width = bucket_width - MARGIN

        y = ((y_value - chart['y_min']) /
             (chart['y_max'] - chart['y_min']))

        bar_height = int(y * avail_height)

        canvas.setStrokeColorRGB(0.25, 0.25, 0.625)
        canvas.setFillColorRGB(0.906, 0.906, 0.953)
        canvas.rect(bar_left, bottom, bar_width, bar_height,
                    stroke=True, fill=True)

        left = left + bucket_width
```

Finally, the `line_series.py` module should look like the following:

```
from ...constants import *

def draw(chart, canvas):
    avail_width  = CHART_WIDTH - Y_AXIS_WIDTH - MARGIN
    bucket_width = avail_width / len(chart['x_axis'])

    bottom       = X_AXIS_HEIGHT
    max_top      = CHART_HEIGHT - TITLE_HEIGHT
    avail_height = max_top - bottom

    left   = Y_AXIS_WIDTH
    prev_y = None
    for y_value in chart['series']:
        y = ((y_value - chart['y_min']) /
             (chart['y_max'] - chart['y_min']))

        cur_y = bottom + int(y * avail_height)

        if prev_y != None:
            canvas.setStrokeColorRGB(0.25, 0.25, 0.625)
            canvas.setLineWidth(1)
```

```
        canvas.line(left - bucket_width / 2, prev_y,
                    left + bucket_width / 2, cur_y)

    prev_y = cur_y
    left = left + bucket_width
```

As you can see, these modules look very similar to their PNG versions. Anything we can do with the Python Imaging Library can also be done with ReportLab, as long as we allow for the differences in the ways these two libraries work.

This leaves us with just one more change we have to make to complete our new implementation of the Charter library: we need to update the renderer.py module to make these new PDF renderer modules available. To do this, add the following import statements to the top of this module:

```
from .pdf import title       as title_pdf
from .pdf import x_axis       as x_axis_pdf
from .pdf import y_axis       as y_axis_pdf
from .pdf import bar_series   as bar_series_pdf
from .pdf import line_series  as line_series_pdf
```

Then, in the part of this module where we define the renderers dictionary, create a new pdf entry to the dictionary by adding the following highlighted lines to your code:

```
renderers = {
    ...
    'pdf' : {
        'title'       : title_pdf,
        'x_axis'      : x_axis_pdf,
        'y_axis'      : y_axis_pdf,
        'bar_series'  : bar_series_pdf,
        'line_series' : line_series_pdf
    }
}
```

Once this is done, you've finished refactoring and reimplementing the Charter module. Assuming you haven't made any mistakes, your library should now be able to generate charts in both PNG and PDF format.

Testing the code

To make sure your program works, edit your `test_charter.py` program and change the name of the output file from `chart.png` to `chart.pdf`. If you then run this program, you should end up with a PDF file that contains a high-quality version of your chart:

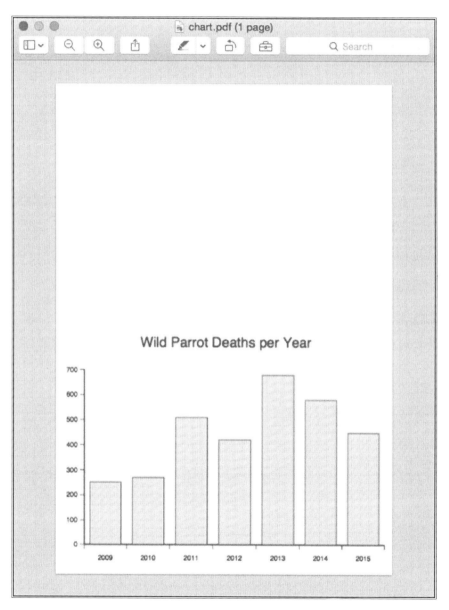

Notice that the chart appears at the bottom of the page, rather than the top. This is because PDF files have their y=0 position at the bottom of the page. You could easily move the chart to the top of the page by calculating the height of the page (in points) and adding an appropriate offset. Feel free to implement this if you want, but for now our task is complete.

If you zoom in, you'll see that the chart's text still looks good:

This is because we're now generating a vector-format PDF file rather than a bitmapped image. This file can be printed on a high-quality laser printer without any pixelation. Even better, existing users of your library will still be able to request PNG versions of the charts and they won't notice any changes at all.

Congratulations—you did it!

Lessons learned

While the Charter library is just an example of modular Python programming, and you don't really have a boss who insists you generate charts in PDF format, these examples were selected because the problem is anything but trivial, and the changes you needed to make were also very challenging. Looking back over what we have achieved, there are several things you may notice:

- When faced with a major change in requirements, our first reaction is usually a negative one: "Oh no! How could I possibly do that?,"a "It'll never work," and so on.

- Rather than jumping in and starting to tinker with the code, it is generally better to step back and think about the structure of the existing code base and what might need to be changed to meet the new requirements.

- Where the new requirement involves a library or tool you haven't used before, it is worth spending some time researching the possible options, and possibly writing a simple example program to check that the library will do what you want, before you start updating your code.

- Through the judicious use of modules and packages, the changes needed to your existing code can be kept to a minimum. In Charter, we could make use of all our existing renderer modules, with only a minor change to the source code. We only had to rewrite one function (the `generate_chart()` function), and add a new `renderer` module to simplify access to our renderers, before writing a new PDF version of each renderer. In this way, the use of modular programming techniques helped to isolate the changes to just the affected parts of the program.

- As often happens, the resulting system is better than the one we started with. Rather than turning our program into spaghetti code, the requirement to support PDF generation resulted in a more modular and better structured library. In particular, the `renderer` module dealt with the complexity of rendering the various chart elements in various formats, allowing the rest of the system to simply call `renderer.draw()` to do the work rather than having to import and use lots of modules directly. Because of this change, we can easily add more chart elements, or more output formats, with minimal further changes to our code.

The overall lesson here is clear: rather than resist changes to your requirements, embrace them. The end result is a better system—more robust, more expandable, and often better organized. Provided, of course, that you do it right.

Summary

In this chapter, we used modular programming techniques to implement a hypothetical chart-generation package called Charter. We saw how charts are made up of standard elements, and how this organization can be translated into program code. After successfully creating a working chart-generation library that renders charts as bitmapped images, we saw how a fundamental change in requirements can seem to be a problem at first, but is actually an opportunity to refactor and improve your code.

Following through with this hypothetical example, we refactored the Charter library to handle PDF formatted charts. In doing so, we learned that using modular techniques to respond to a major change in requirements can help to isolate the changes that need to be made, and that refactoring our code often results in a system that is better organized, more expandable and more robust than what we started with.

In the next chapter, we will learn how to use standard modular programming "patterns" to deal with a range of programming challenges.

5
Working with
Module Patterns

In the previous chapters, we have looked in detail at how Python modules and packages work, and learned how you can use them in your programs. When using modular programming techniques, you will find that the ways in which modules and packages are used tend to follow standard patterns. In this chapter, we will examine a number of these common patterns for using modules and packages to deal with a range of programming challenges. In particular, we will:

- Learn how the divide and conquer technique helps you to solve programming problems

- See how the principle of abstraction helps you to separate what you want to do from how you do it

- Discover how encapsulation allows you to hide the details of how information is represented from the rest of your system

- See that wrappers are modules that call other modules to simplify or alter the way a module is used

- Learn how to create extensible modules

Let's start by looking at the principle of divide and conquer.

Divide and conquer

Divide and conquer is the process of breaking a problem down into smaller parts. You might not know how to solve a particular problem, but by breaking it down into smaller parts, you can then solve each part in turn, which then solves the original problem.

This is a very general technique, of course, and doesn't just apply to the use of modules and packages. However, modular programming helps you work through the divide and conquer process: as you break your problem down, you discover that you'll need a part of your program which performs a given task or range of tasks, and Python modules (and packages) are the perfect way of organizing those tasks.

We have done this several times already in this book. For example, when faced with the challenge of creating a chart-generation library, we used the divide and conquer technique to come up with the notion of a **renderer** that could draw a single chart element. We then realized that we would need several different renderers, which translated perfectly to the `renderers` package containing a separate module for each renderer.

The divide and conquer approach doesn't just suggest a possible modular structure for your code, it works the other way around too. As you think about the design for your program, you may come up with the notion of a module or package that does something related to the problem you're trying to solve. You might even map out the individual functions that each module and package provides. Even though you don't yet know how to solve the whole problem, this modular design helps you to clarify your thinking about the problem, which in turn makes it easier to use the divide-and-conquer approach to solve the remainder of the problem. In other words, modules and packages help you to *clarify your thinking* as you work through the divide and conquer process.

Abstraction

Abstraction is another very general programming pattern that applies to more than just modular programming. Abstraction is essentially the process of hiding complexity: separating *what* you want to do from *how* to do it.

Abstraction is absolutely fundamental to all computer programming. Imagine, for example, that you had to write a program that calculates two averages and then figures out the difference between the two. A simplistic implementation of this program might look something like the following:

```
values_1 = [...]
values_2 = [...]

total_1 = 0
for value in values_1:
    total = total + value
average_1 = total / len(values_1)

total_2 = 0
```

```
for value in values_2:
    total = total + value
average_2 = total / len(values_2)

difference = abs(total_1 - total-2)
print(difference)
```

As you can see, the code that calculates the average of a list of numbers is repeated twice. This is inefficient, so you would normally write a function to avoid repeating yourself. This can be done in the following way:

```
values_1 = [...]
values_2 = [...]

def average(values):
    total = 0
    for value in values:
        total = total + value
    return = total / len(values)

average_1 = average(values_1)
average_2 = average(values_2)
difference = abs(total_1 - total-2)
print(difference)
```

Of course, you do this sort of thing every time you program, but it is actually quite an important process. When you create a function like this, the code inside the function deals with *how* to do something, while the code that calls that function simply knows *what* has to be done—and that the function will do it. In other words, the function *hides the complexity* of how the task is performed, allowing other parts of your program to simply call that function whenever they want that task to be performed.

This type of process is called **abstraction**. Using this pattern, you *abstract away* the details of how something is done so that the rest of your program doesn't need to worry about it.

Abstraction doesn't just apply to writing functions. The general principle of hiding complexity applies to groups of functions as well—and the module is a perfect way of grouping functions together. For example, your program might need to work with colors, and so you write a module named `colors` which contains various functions that allow you to create and work with color values. The various functions in the `colors` module know about color values and how to use them, so the rest of your program doesn't need to worry about it. Using this module, you could do all sorts of interesting things with colors. For example:

```
purple = colors.new_color(1.0, 0.0, 1.0)
yellow = colors.new_color(1.0, 1.0, 0.0)
dark_purple = colors.darken(purple, 0.3)
color_range = colors.blend(yellow, dark_purple, num_steps=20)
dimmed_yellow = colors.desaturate(yellow, 0.8)
```

Outside of this module, your code can simply concentrate on what it wants to do, without the slightest idea of how these various tasks are performed. By doing this, you are using the abstraction pattern to hide away the complexity of these color calculations from the rest of your program.

Abstraction is a fundamental technique for designing and writing modules and packages. For example, the Pillow library we used in the previous chapter provides a wide range of modules that allow you to load, manipulate, create, and save images. We can use this library without having any idea how these various operations are performed. For example, we could call `drawer.line((x1, y1), (x2, y2), color, width)` and not have to worry about the details of setting individual pixels within the image.

One of the great things about applying the abstraction pattern is that you often don't know just how complex something will be when you first start implementing your code. For example, imagine that you are writing a point-of-sale system for a hotel bar. Part of your system will need to calculate the price to charge a customer for the drinks they order. There are various formulae we can use to calculate this price, based on the quantity, the type of liquor used, and so on. But one of the challenging features is the need to support *happy hour*, that is, a period of time during which drinks will be offered at a discounted rate.

At first, you are told that happy hour is between five and six each evening. So, using good modular techniques, you add the following function to your code:

```
def is_happy_hour():
    if datetime.datetime.now().hour == 17: # 5pm.
        return True
    else:
        return False
```

You can then use this function to separate how happy hour is calculated from what happens during happy hour. For example:

```
if is_happy_hour():
    price = price * 0.5
```

So far this is pretty simple, and you might be tempted to bypass the creation of the `is_happy_hour()` function completely. However, this function soon becomes more complicated when you discover that happy hour doesn't apply on Sundays. So, you have to modify the `is_happy_hour()` function to support this:

```
def is_happy_hour():
    if datetime.date.today().weekday() == 6: # Sunday.
        return False
    elif datetime.datetime.now().hour == 17: # 5pm.
        return True
    else:
        return False
```

But you then discover that happy hour doesn't apply on Christmas day or on Good Friday. While Christmas day is easy enough to calculate, the logic used to calculate when Easter is on a given year is much more complicated. If you're interested, the example code for this chapter includes an implementation of the `is_happy_hour()` function which includes support for Christmas day and Good Friday. Needless to say, the implementation is rather complex.

Notice that our `is_happy_hour()` function becomes more and more complicated as we go along — we thought it would be quite simple at first but added requirements made it much more complicated. Fortunately, because we've abstracted away the details of how happy hour is calculated from the code that needs to know whether it is currently happy hour or not, only that one function needs to be updated to support this increased complexity.

Encapsulation

Encapsulation is another programming pattern that often applies to modules and packages. Using encapsulation, you have a *thing* — for example, a color, a customer, or a currency — that you need to store data about, but you hide the representation of this data from the rest of your system. Rather than make the thing available directly, you provide functions for setting, retrieving, and manipulating the thing's data.

To see how this works, let's look back at a module we wrote in the previous chapter. Our chart.py module lets the user define a chart and set the various pieces of information about it. Here is a copy of the code that we wrote for this module:

```
def new_chart():
    return {}

def set_title(chart, title):
    chart['title'] = title

def set_x_axis(chart, x_axis):
    chart['x_axis'] = x_axis

def set_y_axis(chart, minimum, maximum, labels):
    chart['y_min']    = minimum
    chart['y_max']    = maximum
    chart['y_labels'] = labels

def set_series_type(chart, series_type):
    chart['series_type'] = series_type

def set_series(chart, series):
    chart['series'] = series
```

As you can see, the new_chart() function creates a new "chart" without making it clear to the rest of the system how the information about a chart is to be stored—we're using a dictionary here, but we could just as easily have used an object, a base64-encoded string, or whatever. The rest of the system doesn't care as it simply calls the various functions within the chart.py module to set the various values for a chart.

Unfortunately, this isn't quite a perfect example of encapsulation. Our various set_XXX() functions act as **setters**—they let us set the various values for a chart— but we just assume that our chart-generation functions can access the information about a chart directly from the chart's dictionary. If this was going to be a pure example of encapsulation, we would also write the equivalent **getter** functions, for example:

```
def get_title(chart):
    return chart['title']

def get_x_axis(chart):
    return chart['x_axis']

def get_y_axis(chart):
```

```
    return (chart['y_min'], chart['y_max'], chart['y_labels'])

def get_series_type(chart):
    return chart['series_type']

def get_series(chart):
    return chart['series']
```

With these getter functions added to our module, we now have a fully encapsulated module that allows us to store and retrieve information about a chart. The other parts of the `charter` package that want to use a chart would then call the getter functions to retrieve that chart's data, rather than accessing it directly.

> These examples of writing setter and getter functions in a module are slightly contrived; encapsulation is usually done using object-oriented programming techniques. However, as you can see, it is perfectly possible to use encapsulation when writing code that uses only modular programming techniques.

You might be wondering why on earth anyone would want to use encapsulation. Instead of writing `charts.get_title(chart)`, why not simply write `chart['title']`? The second version is shorter. It also avoids calling a function and so would be infinitesimally faster. Why bother with encapsulation at all?

There are two reasons why you should use encapsulation in your programs. Firstly, by using getter and setter functions, you hide the details of how your information is stored. This allows you to change the internal representation without affecting any other part of your program—and the one thing you can pretty much guarantee as you write your program is that you're going to be adding more information and features as you go along. This means that the internal representation of your data *will* change. By separating what you are storing from how it is stored, your system becomes more robust, and you can make changes without having to rewrite a lot of code. This is the hallmark of a good modular design.

The second major reason for using encapsulation is to allow your code to do something when the user sets a particular value. For example, if the user changes the quantity of an order, you can immediately recalculate the total price for that order. Another thing that setters often do is save the updated value to disk or into a database. You can also add error-checking and other logic to your setters in order to catch bugs that might otherwise be hard to track down.

Let's take a detailed look at a Python module that uses the encapsulation pattern. For this example, let's pretend that we are writing a program for storing recipes. The user can create a database of favorite recipes and display these recipes when they want to use them.

Let's create a Python module to encapsulate the concept of a recipe. For this example, we'll store the recipe in memory to keep things simple. For each recipe, we will store the name, the number of servings the recipe produces, a list of ingredients, and a list of instructions the user needs to follow when making the recipe.

Create a new Python source file, named `recipes.py`, and enter the following into this file:

```python
def new():
    return {'name'          : None,
            'num_servings'  : 1,
            'instructions'  : [],
            'ingredients'   : []}

def set_name(recipe, name):
    recipe['name'] = name

def get_name(recipe):
    return recipe['name']

def set_num_servings(recipe, num_servings):
    recipe['num_servings'] = num_servings

def get_num_servings(recipe):
    return recipe['num_servings']

def set_ingredients(recipe, ingredients):
    recipe['ingredients'] = ingredients

def get_ingredients(recipe):
    return recipe['ingredients']

def set_instructions(recipe, instructions):
    recipe['instructions'] = instructions

def get_instructions(recipe):
    return recipe['instructions']

def add_instruction(recipe, instruction):
```

```
        recipe['instructions'].append(instruction)

    def add_ingredient(recipe, ingredient, amount, units):
        recipe['ingredients'].append({'ingredient' : ingredient,
                                      'amount'     : amount,
                                      'units'      : units})
```

As you can see, we are once again using a Python dictionary to store our information. We could use a Python class or a `namedtuple` from the Python Standard Library. Alternatively, we could store our information in a database. For this example, however, we want to keep our code as simple as possible, and a dictionary is the easiest solution.

After creating a new recipe, the user can call the various setter and getter functions to store and retrieve information about the recipe. We also have some helpful functions that let us add the instructions and ingredients one at a time, which is more convenient for the program we are writing.

Notice that when adding an ingredient to the recipe, the caller needs to supply three pieces of information: the name of the ingredient, the required quantity, and the units in which this quantity is measured. For example:

```
    recipes.add_ingredient(recipe, "Milk", 1, "cup")
```

So far, we have encapsulated the concept of a recipe, allowing us to store the information we need and retrieve it when required. Because our module followed the encapsulation principle, we could change the way recipes are stored, add more information, and new behavior to our module without affecting the rest of the program.

Let's add one more useful function to our recipe:

```
    def to_string(recipe, num_servings):
        multiplier = num_servings / recipe['num_servings']
        s = []
        s.append("Recipe for {}, {} servings:".format(recipe['name'],
                                                        num_servings))
        s.append("")
        s.append("Ingredients:")
        s.append("")
        for ingredient in recipe['ingredients']:
            s.append("    {} - {} {}".format(
                        ingredient['ingredient'],
                        ingredient['amount'] * multiplier,
                        ingredient['units']))
        s.append("")
```

```
        s.append("Instructions:")
        s.append("")
        for i,instruction in enumerate(recipe['instructions']):
            s.append("{}. {}".format(i+1, instruction))

        return s
```

This function returns a list of strings which can be printed out to summarize the recipe. Notice the num_servings parameter: this allows us to customize the recipe for a different number of servings. For example, if the user creates a recipe for three servings and wants to double it, the to_string() function can be called with a num_servings value of 6, and the correct quantities will be included in the list of returned strings.

Let's take a look at how this module works. Open up a terminal or command-line window, use the cd command to go to the directory where you created your recipes.py file, and type python to start the Python interpreter. Then, try typing the following to create a recipe for pizza dough:

```
import recipes

recipe = recipes.new("Pizza Dough", num_servings=1)

recipes.add_ingredient(recipe, "Greek Yogurt", 1, "cup")

recipes.add_ingredient(recipe, "Self-Raising Flour", 1.5, "cups")

recipes.add_instruction(recipe, "Combine yogurt and 2/3 of the flour in a
bowl and mix with a beater until combined")

recipes.add_instruction(recipe, "Slowly add additional flour until it
forms a stiff dough")

recipes.add_instruction(recipe, "Turn out onto a floured surface and
knead until dough is tacky")

recipes.add_instruction(recipe, "Roll out into a circle of the desired
thickness and place on a greased and lined baking tray")
```

So far so good. Let's now use the to_string() function to print out the details of the recipe, doubling it to two servings:

```
for s in recipes.to_string(recipe, num_servings=2):
    print s
```

All going well, the recipe should be printed out for you:

```
Recipe for Pizza Dough, 2 servings:


Ingredients:

    Greek Yogurt - 2 cup
    Self-rising Flour - 3.0 cups


Instructions:


1. Combine yogurt and 2/3 of the flour in a bowl and mix with a beater
until combined

2. Slowly add additional flour until it forms a stiff dough

3. Turn out onto a floured surface and knead until dough is tacky

4. Roll out into a circle of the desired thickness and place on a greased
and lined baking tray
```

As you can see, there are a few minor formatting issues. For example, the required quantity of Greek yogurt is listed as `2  cup` rather than `2  cups`. You can fix this easily enough if you want—but the important thing to notice is that the `recipes.py` module has encapsulated the idea of a recipe, allowing you (and other programs you write) to work with recipes without having to worry about the details.

As an exercise, you might like to try fixing the display of quantities in the `to_string()` function. You could also try writing a new function that creates a shopping list from a list of recipes, automatically combining quantities when two or more recipes use the same ingredient. If you work through these exercises, you'll soon notice that the implementation can get quite complicated, but by encapsulating the details in a module, you can hide these details from the rest of your program.

Wrappers

A wrapper is essentially a group of functions that call other functions to do the work:

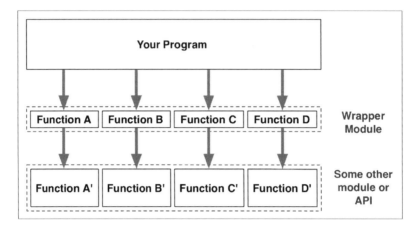

Wrappers are used to simplify an interface, to make a confusing or badly designed API easier to use, to convert data formats into something more convenient, and to implement cross-language compatibility. Wrappers are also sometimes used to add testing and error-checking code to an existing API.

Let's take a look at a real-world application of a wrapper module. Imagine that you work for a large bank and have been asked to write a program to analyze fund transfers to help identify possible fraud. Your program receives information, in real time, about every inter-bank funds transfer that takes place. For each transfer, you are given:

- The amount of the transfer
- The ID of the branch in which the transfer took place
- The identification code for the bank the funds are being sent to

Your task is to analyze the transfers over time to identify unusual patterns of activity. To do this, you need to calculate, for each of the last eight days, the total value of all transfers for each branch and destination bank. You can then compare the current day's totals against the average for the previous seven days, and flag any daily totals that are more than 50% above the average.

You start by deciding how to represent the total transfers for a day. Because you need to keep track of this for each branch and destination bank, it makes sense to store these totals in a two-dimensional array:

Branch ID	Destination Bank Code					
	AMERUS33	CERYUS33	EQTYUS44	LOYDUS33	SYNEUS44	WFBIUS6S
125000249	--	$307,512	$1,612	--	$43,902	$5,602,918
125000252	$79,400	$3,416,710	$75	$23,508	$60,912	$5,806
125000371	$88,400	--	$7,718	$50,412	$102,519	$612,510
125000402	$8,190	$66,402,010	$92,000	$578	$1,402,620	--
125000596	$102,416	$808,908	$50,000	$17,400	$38,502	$2,048
125001067	$16,400	$1,643,802	--	$2,340	$77,841	$17,024

In Python, this type of two-dimensional array is represented as a list of lists:

```
totals = [[0, 307512, 1612, 0, 43902, 5602918],
          [79400, 3416710, 75, 23508, 60912, 5806],
          ...
         ]
```

You can then keep a separate list of the branch ID for each row and another list holding the destination bank code for each column:

```
branch_ids = [125000249, 125000252, 125000371, ...]
bank_codes = ["AMERUS33", "CERYUS33", "EQTYUS44", ...]
```

Using these lists, you can calculate the totals for a given day by processing the transfers that took place on that particular day:

```
totals = []
for branch in branch_ids:
    branch_totals = []
    for bank in bank_codes:
        branch_totals.append(0)
    totals.append(branch_totals)

for transfer in transfers_for_day:
    branch_index = branch_ids.index(transfer['branch'])
    bank_index   = bank_codes.index(transfer['dest_bank'])
    totals[branch_index][bank_index] += transfer['amount']
```

So far so good. Once you have these totals for each day, you can then calculate the average and compare it against the current day's totals to identify the entries that are higher than 150% of the average.

Let's imagine that you've written this program and managed to get it working. When you start using it, though, you immediately discover a problem: your bank has over 5,000 branches, and there are more than 15,000 banks worldwide that your bank can transfer funds to—that's a total of 75 million combinations that you need to keep totals for, and as a result, your program is taking far too long to calculate the totals.

To make your program faster, you need to find a better way of handling large arrays of numbers. Fortunately, there's a library designed to do just this: **NumPy**.

NumPy is an excellent array-handling library. You can create huge arrays and perform sophisticated operations on an array with a single function call. Unfortunately, NumPy is also a dense and impenetrable library. It was designed and written for people with a deep understanding of mathematics. While there are many tutorials available and you can generally figure out how to use it, the code that uses NumPy is often hard to comprehend. For example, to calculate the average across multiple matrices would involve the following:

```
daily_totals = []
for totals in totals_to_average:
    daily_totals.append(totals)
average = numpy.mean(numpy.array(daily_totals), axis=0)
```

Figuring out what that last line does would require a trip to the NumPy documentation. Because of the complexity of the code that uses NumPy, this is a perfect example of a situation where a **wrapper module** can be used: the wrapper module can provide an easier-to-use interface to NumPy, so your code can use it without being cluttered with complex and confusing function calls.

To work through this example, we'll start by installing the NumPy library. NumPy (`http://www.numpy.org`) runs on Mac OS X, Windows, and Linux machines. How you install it depends on which operating system you are using:

- For Mac OS X, you can download an installer from `http://www.kyngchaos.com/software/python`.

- For MS Windows, you can download a Python "wheel" file for NumPy from `http://www.lfd.uci.edu/~gohlke/pythonlibs/#numpy`. Choose the pre-built version of NumPy that matches your operating system and the desired version of Python. To use the wheel file, use the `pip install` command, for example, `pip install numpy-1.10.4+mkl-cp34-none-win32.whl`.

   For more information about installing Python wheels, refer to `https://pip.pypa.io/en/latest/user_guide/#installing-from-wheels`.

- If your computer runs Linux, you can use your Linux package manager to install NumPy. Alternatively, you can download and build NumPy in source code form.

To ensure that NumPy is working, fire up your Python interpreter and enter the following:

```
import numpy
a = numpy.array([[1, 2], [3, 4]])
print(a)
```

All going well, you should see a 2 x 2 matrix displayed:

```
[[1 2]
 [3 4]]
```

Now that we have NumPy installed, let's start working on our wrapper module. Create a new Python source file, named `numpy_wrapper.py`, and enter the following into this file:

```
import numpy
```

That's all for now; we'll add functions to this wrapper module as we need them.

Next, create another Python source file, named `detect_unusual_transfers.py`, and enter the following into this file:

```
import random
import numpy_wrapper as npw


BANK_CODES = ["AMERUS33", "CERYUS33", "EQTYUS44",
              "LOYDUS33", "SYNEUS44", "WFBIUS6S"]


BRANCH_IDS = ["125000249", "125000252", "125000371",
              "125000402", "125000596", "125001067"]
```

As you can see, we are hardwiring the bank and branch codes for our example; in a real program, these values would be loaded from somewhere, such as a file or a database. Since we don't have any available data, we will use the `random` module to create some. We are also changing the name of the `numpy_wrapper` module to make it easier to access from our code.

Let's now create some funds transfer data to process, using the `random` module:

```
days = [1, 2, 3, 4, 5, 6, 7, 8]
transfers = []

for i in range(10000):
    day       = random.choice(days)
    bank_code = random.choice(BANK_CODES)
    branch_id = random.choice(BRANCH_IDS)
    amount    = random.randint(1000, 1000000)

    transfers.append((day, bank_code, branch_id, amount))
```

Here, we randomly select a day, a bank code, a branch ID, and an amount, storing these values in the `transfers` list.

Our next task is to collate this information into a series of arrays. This allows us to calculate the total value of the transfers for each day, grouped by the branch ID and destination bank. To do this, we'll create a NumPy array for each day, where the rows in each array represent branches and the columns represent destination banks. We'll then go through the list of transfers, processing them one by one. The following illustration summarizes how we process each transfer in turn:

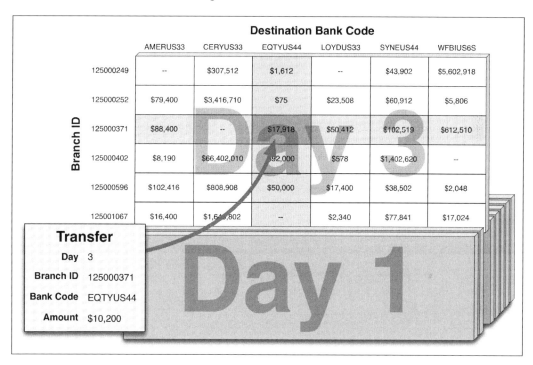

First, we select the array for the day on which the transfer occurred, and then we select the appropriate row and column based on the destination bank and the branch ID. Finally, we add the amount of the transfer to that item within the day's array.

Let's implement this logic. Our first task is to create a series of NumPy arrays, one for each day. Here, we immediately hit a snag: NumPy has many different options for creating arrays; in this case, we want to create an array that holds integer values and has its contents initialized to zero. If we used NumPy directly, our code would look like the following:

```
array = numpy.zeros((num_rows, num_cols), dtype=numpy.int32)
```

This is not exactly easy to understand, so we're going to move this logic into our NumPy wrapper module. Edit the numpy_wrapper.py file, and add the following to the end of this module:

```
def new(num_rows, num_cols):
    return numpy.zeros((num_rows, num_cols), dtype=numpy.int32)
```

Now, we can create a new array by calling our wrapper function (npw.new()) and not have to worry about the details of how NumPy works at all. We have simplified the interface to this particular aspect of NumPy:

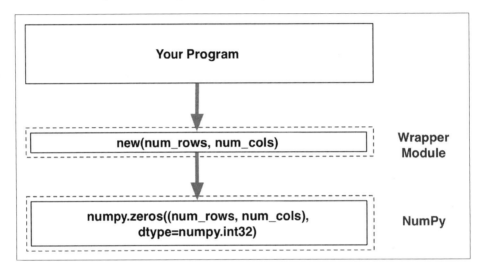

Let's now use our wrapper function to create the eight arrays that we will need, one for each day. Add the following to the end of the detect_unusual_transfers.py file:

```
transfers_by_day = {}
for day in days:
    transfers_by_day[day] = npw.new(num_rows=len(BANK_CODES),
                                    num_cols=len(BRANCH_IDS))
```

Now that we have our NumPy arrays, we can use them as if they were nested Python lists. For example:

```
array[row][col] = array[row][col] + amount
```

We just need to choose the appropriate array, and calculate the row and column numbers to use. Here is the necessary code, which you should add to the end of your `detect_unusual_transfers.py` script:

```
for day,bank_code,branch_id,amount in transfers:
    array = transfers_by_day[day]
    row = BRANCH_IDS.index(branch_id)
    col = BANK_CODES.index(bank_code)
    array[row][col] = array[row][col] + amount
```

Now that we've collated the transfers into eight NumPy arrays, we want to use all this data to detect any unusual activity. For each combination of branch ID and destination bank code, we will need to do the following:

1. Calculate the average of the first seven days' activity.
2. Multiply the calculated average by 1.5.
3. If the activity on the eighth day is greater than the average multiplied by 1.5, then we consider this activity to be unusual.

Of course, we need to do this for every row and column in our arrays, which would be very slow; this is why we're using NumPy. So, we need to calculate the average for multiple arrays of numbers, then multiply the array of averages by 1.5, and finally, compare the values within the multiplied array against the array for the eighth day of data. Fortunately, these are all things that NumPy can do for us.

We'll start by collecting together the seven arrays we need to average, as well as the array for the eighth day. To do this, add the following to the end of your program:

```
latest_day = max(days)

transfers_to_average = []
for day in days:
    if day != latest_day:
        transfers_to_average.append(transfers_by_day[day])

current = transfers_by_day[latest_day]
```

To calculate the average of a list of arrays, NumPy requires us to use the following function call:

```
average = numpy.mean(numpy.array(arrays_to_average), axis=0)
```

Since this is confusing, we will move this function into our wrapper. Add the following code to the end of the `numpy_wrapper.py` module:

```
def average(arrays_to_average):
    return numpy.mean(numpy.array(arrays_to_average), axis=0)
```

This lets us calculate the average of the seven day's activity using a single call to our wrapper function. To do this, add the following to the end of your `detect_unusual_transfers.py` script:

```
average = npw.average(transfers_to_average)
```

As you can see, using the wrapper makes our code much easier to understand.

Our next task is to multiply the array of calculated averages by 1.5, and compare the result against the current day's totals. Fortunately, NumPy makes this easy:

```
unusual_transfers = current > average * 1.5
```

Because this code is so clear, there's no advantage in creating a wrapper function for it. The resulting array, `unusual_transfers`, will be the same size as our `current` and `average` arrays, where each entry in the array is either `True` or `False`:

False	False	False	False	False	False
False	False	False	True	False	False
False	False	False	False	False	False
False	False	False	False	False	False
False	True	False	False	False	False
False	False	False	False	False	False

We're almost done; our final task is to identify the array entries with a value of `True`, and tell the user about the unusual activity. While we could scan through every row and column to find the `True` entries, using NumPy is much faster. The following NumPy code will give us a list containing the row and column numbers for the `True` entries in the array:

```
indices = numpy.transpose(array.nonzero())
```

True to form, though, this code is hard to understand, so it's a perfect candidate for another wrapper function. Go back to your `numpy_wrapper.py` module, and add the following to the end of the file:

```
def get_indices(array):
    return numpy.transpose(array.nonzero())
```

This function returns a list (actually an array) of `(row,col)` values for all the `True` entries in the array. Back in our `detect_unusual_activity.py` file, we can use this function to quickly identify the unusual activity:

```
for row,col in npw.get_indices(unusual_transfers):
    branch_id   = BRANCH_IDS[row]
    bank_code   = BANK_CODES[col]
    average_amt = int(average[row][col])
    current_amt = current[row][col]

    print("Branch {} transferred ${:,d}".format(branch_id,
                                                 current_amt) +
          " to bank {}, average = ${:,d}".format(bank_code,
                                                 average_amt))
```

As you can see, we use the `BRANCH_IDS` and `BANK_CODES` lists to convert from the row and column number back to the relevant branch ID and bank code. We also retrieve the average and current amounts for the suspicious activity. Finally, we print out this information to warn the user about the unusual activity.

If you run your program, you should see an output that looks something like this:

```
Branch 125000371 transferred $24,729,847 to bank WFBIUS6S, average =
$14,954,617
Branch 125000402 transferred $26,818,710 to bank CERYUS33, average =
$16,338,043
Branch 125001067 transferred $27,081,511 to bank EQTYUS44, average =
$17,763,644
```

Because we are using random numbers for our financial data, the output will be random too. Try running the program a few times; you may not get any output at all if none of the randomly-generated values are suspicious.

Of course, we are not really interested in detecting suspicious financial activity — this example is just an excuse for working with NumPy. What is far more interesting is the wrapper module that we created, hiding the complexity of the NumPy interface so that the rest of our program can concentrate on the job to be done.

If we were to continue developing our unusual activity detector, we would no doubt add more functionality to our `numpy_wrapper.py` module as we found more NumPy functions that we wanted to wrap.

This is just one example of a wrapper module. As we mentioned earlier, simplifying a complex and confusing API is just one use for a wrapper module; they can also be used to convert data from one format to another, add testing and error-checking code to an existing API, and call functions that are written in a different language.

Note that, by definition, a wrapper is always *thin* — while there might be code in a wrapper (for example, to convert a parameter from an object into a dictionary), the wrapper function always ends up calling another function to do the actual work.

Extensible modules

Most of the time, the functionality provided by a module is known in advance. The module's source code implements a well-defined set of behavior, and that is all the module does. In some situations, however, you may need a module where the behavior of the module is not completely defined at the time you write it. Other parts of your system can *extend* the behavior of the module in various ways. Modules that are designed to be extended are called **extensible modules**.

One of the great things about Python is that it is a *dynamic* language. You don't need to define and compile all your code before it will run. This makes it easy to create extensible modules using Python.

In this section, we will look at three different ways in which a module can be made extensible: through the use of **dynamic imports**, by writing **plugins**, and using **hooks**.

Dynamic imports

In the previous chapter, we created a module called `renderers.py` which selected an appropriate renderer module to draw a chart element using a given output format. The following is an abbreviated copy of this module's source code:

```
from .png import title  as title_png
from .png import x_axis as x_axis_png

from .pdf import title  as title_pdf
from .pdf import x_axis as x_axis_pdf

renderers = {
    'png' : {
        'title' : title_png,
```

```
        'x_axis' : x_axis_png,
    },
    'pdf' : {
        'title'  : title_pdf,
        'x_axis' : x_axis_pdf,
    }
}


def draw(format, element, chart, output):
    renderers[format][element].draw(chart, output)
```

This module is interesting because it implements, in a limited way, the concept of extensibility. Notice that the `renderer.draw()` function calls a `draw()` function within another module to do the actual work; which module is used depends on the desired chart format and the element to be drawn.

This module is not truly extensible because the list of possible modules is determined by the `import` statements at the top of the module. However, it is possible to turn this into a fully extensible module by making use of `importlib`. This is a module in the Python Standard Library that gives a developer access to the internal mechanism used to import modules; using `importlib`, you can import modules dynamically.

To understand how this works, let's look at an example. Create a new directory to hold your source code, and in this directory, create a new module named `module_a.py`. Enter the following code into this module:

```
def say_hello():
    print("Hello from module_a")
```

Now, create a copy of this module, named `module_b.py`, and edit the `say_hello()` function to print *Hello from module_b*. Then, repeat the process to create `module_c.py`.

We now have three modules that all implement a function named `say_hello()`. Now, create another Python source file in the same directory, and name it `load_module.py`. Then, enter the following into this file:

```
import importlib

module_name = input("Load module: ")
if module_name != "":
    module = importlib.import_module(module_name)
    module.say_hello()
```

This program prompts the user to enter a string using the `input()` statement. We then call `importlib.import_module()` to import the module with that name, and call that module's `say_hello()` function.

Try running this program, and when prompted, type in `module_a`. You should see the following message displayed:

`Hello from module_a`

Try repeating this process with the other modules. If you type in the name of a non-existent module, you'll get an `ImportError`.

Of course, `importlib` isn't limited to importing modules in the same directory as the current module; you can include package names if you want. For example:

```
module = importlib.import_module("package.sub_package.module")
```

Using `importlib`, you can import a module dynamically—you don't need to know the name of the module at the time you write your program. We could use this to rewrite the `renderer.py` module from the previous chapter to make it fully extensible:

```
from importlib import import_module


def draw(format, element, chart, output):
    renderer = import_module("{}.{}.{}".format(__package__,
                                               format,
                                               element))
    renderer.draw(chart, output)
```

 Notice the use of the special `__package__` variable. This holds the name of the package enclosing the current module; using this allows us to import a module relative to the package that the `renderer.py` module is part of.

The great thing about dynamic imports is that you don't need to know what all the modules are at the time you create your program. Using the `renderer.py` example, you could add new chart formats or elements by creating new renderer modules, and the system will import them when requested, without having to make any changes at all to your `renderer.py` module.

Plugins

Plugins are modules that the user (or another developer) writes and "plugs in" to your program. Plugins are popular in many large systems such as WordPress, JQuery, Google Chrome, and Adobe Photoshop. Plugins are used to extend the functionality of an existing program.

In Python, it is easy to implement plugins using the same dynamic import mechanism we discussed in the previous section. The only difference is that instead of importing modules that are already part of your program's source code, you set up a separate directory where the user can place the plugins they want to add to your program. This could be as simple as creating a `plugins` directory at the top level of your program, or you could store your plugins in a directory outside of your program's source code, and modify `sys.path` so that the Python interpreter can find the modules in that directory. Either way, your program will use `importlib.import_module()` to load the desired plugin, and then access the functions and other definitions within the plugin just like you would access functions and other definitions in any other Python module.

The sample code available for this chapter includes a simple plugin loader which shows how this mechanism works.

Hooks

A **hook** is a way of allowing external code to be called at particular points in your program. A hook is usually a function—your program checks to see if a hook function has been defined, and if so, it calls this function at an appropriate time.

Let's look at a concrete example. Imagine that you have a program that includes the ability to log a user in and out. Part of your program may include the following module, which we will call `login_module.py`:

```python
cur_user = None

def login(username, password):
    if is_password_correct(username, password):
        cur_user = username
        return True
    else:
        return False

def logout():
    cur_user = None
```

Now, imagine that you want to add a hook that gets called whenever the user logs in. Adding this to your program would involve the following changes to this module:

```python
cur_user = None
login_hook = None

def set_login_hook(hook):
```

```
        login_hook = hook

    def login(username, password):
        if is_password_correct(username, password):
            cur_user = username
            if login_hook != None:
                login_hook(username)
            return True
        else:
            return False

    def logout():
        cur_user = None
```

With this code in place, other parts of your system can hook into your login process by setting their own login hook function, which does something whenever the user logs in. For example:

```
    def my_login_hook(username):
        if user_has_messages(username):
            show_messages(username)

    login_module.set_login_hook(my_login_hook)
```

By implementing this login hook, you have extended the behavior of the login process without altering the login module itself.

There are a couple of things to be aware of with hooks:

- Depending on the behavior you are implementing a hook for, the value returned by the hook function might be used to alter the behavior of your code. For example, if the login hook returned `False`, the user might be blocked from logging in. This doesn't apply to every hook, but it can be a very useful way of giving a hook function more control over what happens in your program.

- In this example, we only allow a single hook function to be defined for each hook. Another way of implementing this would be to have a list of registered hook functions, and let your program add or remove hook functions as required. In this way, you could have several hook functions, which get called one after the other whenever something happens.

Hooks are an excellent way of adding specific points of extensibility to your modules. They are easy to implement and use, and unlike dynamic imports and plugins, they don't require you to put your code into a separate module. This means that hooks are an ideal way of extending your modules in a very fine-grained way.

Summary

In this chapter, we saw that the ways in which modules and packages are used tend to follow standard patterns. We examined the divide-and-conquer pattern, which is the process of breaking a problem down into smaller parts, and saw how this technique both helps to structure your programs and clarify your thinking about the problem you are trying to solve.

We next looked at the abstraction pattern, which is the process of hiding complexity by separating what you want to do from how to do it. We then examined the notion of encapsulation, which is where you store data about something but hide the details of how that data is represented from the rest of the system, and use getter and setter functions to provide access to that data.

We then turned to the concept of wrappers, and saw how wrappers can be used to simplify the interface to a complex or confusing API, to convert data formats, to implement cross-language compatibility, and to add testing and error-checking code to an existing API.

Finally, we learned about extensible modules, and saw how we can use the techniques of dynamic module imports, plugins, and hooks to create a module that does more than you designed it to do. We saw that the dynamic nature of Python makes it ideally suited to the creation of extensible modules where the behavior of your modules is not completely defined at the time you write them.

In the next chapter, we will learn how to design and implement modules that can be shared and reused in other programs.

6
Creating Reusable Modules

As well as being a good technique for writing programs for your own use, modular programming is also an excellent way of writing programs that can be used by other programmers. In this chapter, we will look at how to design and implement modules and packages that can be shared and reused in other programs. In particular, we will:

- See how modules and packages can be used as a way of sharing the code that you write
- See how writing a module for reuse differs from writing a module for use as part of just one program
- Discover what makes a module suitable for reuse
- Look at examples of successful reusable modules
- Design a package to be reusable
- Implement a reusable package

Let's start by taking a look at how you can use modules and packages to share your code with other people.

Using modules and packages to share your code

Whenever you write some Python source code, the code you create will perform a task of some sort. Maybe your code analyzes some data, stores some information into a file, or prompts the user to choose an item from a list. It doesn't matter what your code is—ultimately, your code does *something*.

Often, this something is very specific. For example, you might have a function that calculates compound interest, generates a Venn diagram, or displays a warning message to the user. Once you've written this code, you can then use it wherever you want in your own program. This is the simply abstraction pattern that was described in the previous chapter: you separate *what* you want to do from *how* you do it.

Once you've written your function, you can then call it whenever you want to perform that task. For example, you can call your `display_warning()` function whenever you want to display a warning to the user, without worrying about the details of how the warning is displayed.

However, this hypothetical `display_warning()` function isn't just useful in the program you are currently writing. Other programs may want to perform the same task—both programs that you write in the future and programs that other people may write. Rather than reinvent the wheel each time, it often makes sense to *reuse* your code.

To reuse your code, you have to share it. Sometimes, you might share your code with yourself so that you can use it within a different program. At other times, you might share your code with other developers so that they can use it within their own programs.

Of course, you don't just share code with others for philanthropic reasons. In a larger organization, you are often required to share code to improve the productivity of your peers. Even if you work by yourself, you will benefit by using code other people have shared and, by sharing your own code, other people can help find bugs and fix problems that you're not able to fix yourself.

Regardless of whether you share your code with yourself (in other projects) or with others (within your organization or in the wider development community), the basic process is the same. There are three main ways in which you can share your code:

1. You can create a code snippet that is then copied and pasted into the new program. The code snippet might be stored in an application called a `Code Snippet Manager` or a folder of text files, or even published as part of a blog.

2. You can place the code you want to share into a module or package, and then import this module or package into the new program. The module or package can be physically copied into the new program's source code, it can be placed in your Python installation's `site-packages` directory, or you can modify `sys.path` to include the directory where the module or package can be found.

3. Alternatively, you can turn your code into a standalone program, and then call this program from other code using `os.system()`.

While all these options work, not all of them are ideal. Let's take a closer look at each one:

- Code snippets are great for short pieces of code that form just part of a function. They're terrible, however, at keeping track of where that code ends up. Because you've copied and pasted the code into the middle of a new program, it is very easy to modify it as there's no easy way of distinguishing the pasted code from the rest of the program you've written. Also, if the original snippet needs to be modified, for example, to fix a bug, you'll have to find where you've used the snippet in your program and update it to match. All of this is rather messy and prone to errors.

- The technique of importing modules or packages has the advantage of working well with larger chunks of code. The code you are sharing can include multiple functions and even be split across multiple source files using a Python package. You are also much less likely to accidentally modify an imported module as the source code is stored in a separate file.

  If you have copied the source module or package across to your new program, then you will need to manually update it if the original is changed. This is not ideal, but since you're replacing whole files, this isn't too difficult. On the other hand, if your new program uses a module stored elsewhere, then there's nothing to update—any changes made to the original module will immediately apply to any programs which use that module.

- Finally, organizing your code into a standalone program means that your new program has to execute it. This can be done in the following way:

```
status = os.system("python other_program.py <params>")
if status != 0:
    print("The other_program failed!")
```

  As you can see, it is possible to run another Python program, wait for it to finish, and then check the returned status code to ensure that the program ran successfully. You can also pass parameters to the running program if you wish. However, the information you can pass to the program and receive back is extremely limited. This approach will work, for example, if you have a program that parses an XML file and saves a summary of this file into a different file on disk, but you can't directly pass Python data structures to another program for processing, and you can't receive Python data structures back again.

 Actually, you *can* transmit Python data structures between running programs, but the process involved is so complicated that it isn't worth considering.

As you can see, snippets, module/package imports, and standalone programs form a kind of continuum: snippets are very small and fine-grained, module and package imports support larger chunks of code while still being easy to use and update, and standalone programs are large but limited in the way you can interact with them.

Of these three, using module and package imports to share code appears to hit the sweet spot: they can be used for large amounts of code, are easy to use and interact with, and are trivially easy to update when necessary. This makes modules and packages the ideal mechanism for sharing your Python source code—both with yourself, for use in future projects, and with other people.

What makes a module reusable?

In order for a module or package to be reusable, it has to meet the following requirements:

- It must function as a standalone unit
- If your package is intended to be included as part of the source code for another system, you must use relative imports to load the other modules within your package
- Any external dependencies must be clearly noted

If a module or package does not meet these three requirements, it would be very hard, if not impossible, to reuse it in other programs. Let's now take a closer look at each of these requirements in turn.

Functioning as a standalone unit

Imagine that you decide to share a module named `encryption`, which performs text encryption using public/private key pairs. Another programmer then copies this module into their program. When they try to use it, however, their program crashes with the following error message:

```
ImportError: No module named 'hash_utils'
```

The `encryption` module may have been shared, but it was dependent on another module within the original program (`hash_utils.py`) that wasn't shared, and so the `encryption` module by itself is useless.

The solution to this problem is to combine the module you want to share with any other modules it may depend upon, putting the modules together into a package. You then share the package, rather than the individual module. The following illustration shows how this might be done:

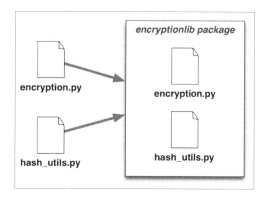

In this example, we have created a new package named `encryptionlib` and moved both the `encryption.py` and `hash_utils.py` files into this package. Of course, this requires you to refactor the rest of your program to allow for the new position of these modules, but it does then allow you to reuse your encryption logic in other programs.

> While it can be a nuisance having to refactor your program in this way, the result is almost always an improvement on your original program. Putting dependent modules together into a package helps to improve the overall organization of your code.

Using relative imports

Continuing with the example from the previous section, imagine that you want to use your new `encryptionlib` package as part of another program, but don't want to make it publically available as a separate package. In this case, you can simply include the entire `encryptionlib` directory as part of your new system's source code. When you do this, however, you can run into problems if your modules don't use relative imports. For example, if your `encryption` module is dependent on the `hash_utils` module, then the `encryption` module is going to include an `import` statement referring to the `hash_utils` module. However, the resulting package cannot be reused if the `encryption` module imports `hash_utils` in any of the following ways:

```
import hash_utils
from my_program.lib import hash_utils
from hash_utils import *
```

All of these import statements will fail because they assume that the `hash_utils.py` file is at a particular fixed point in your program's source code. Any assumption about the position of a dependent module within the program's source code will limit the reusability of the package as you can't then move the package to a different place and expect it to work. Given the requirements of the new project, you will often have to store packages and modules in a different place from where they were originally developed. For example, perhaps the `encryptionlib` package needs to be installed in a `thirdparty` package along with all the other reused libraries. Using absolute imports, your package will fail because the location of the modules within it will have changed.

 This doesn't apply if you publish your package and then install it into your Python `site-packages` directory. However, there are many situations where you don't want to install a reusable package inside the `site-packages` directory, and so you will need to be careful about relative imports.

To solve this problem, make sure that any `import` statements within a package that refer to other modules within the same package always use a relative import. For example:

```
from . import hash_utils
```

This will allow your package to work no matter where in the Python source tree the package has been placed.

Noting external dependencies

Imagine that our new `encryptionlib` package makes use of the `NumPy` library we encountered in the previous chapter. Perhaps `hash_utils` imports some functions from NumPy and uses them to quickly calculate a binary hash of a list of numbers. Even though NumPy was installed as part of the original program, you can't assume that the same is true of the new program: if you were to install the `encryptionlib` package into a new program and run it, it would eventually fail with the following error:

```
ImportError: No module named 'numpy'
```

To prevent this from happening, it is important that anyone wanting to reuse your module is aware of the dependency on a third-party module and knows exactly what needs to be installed for your module or package to function. An ideal place to include this information is in the README file or other documentation for the module or package you are sharing.

> If you are using an automated deployment system such as setuptools or pip, these tools have their own way of identifying your package's requirements. It is still a good idea, though, to list the requirements in your documentation so your users will be aware of them before the package is installed.

What makes a good reusable module?

In the previous section, we looked at the *minimum* requirements for a reusable module. Let's now examine the *ideal* requirements for reusability. What would a perfect reusable module look like?

There are three things that distinguish an excellent reusable module from a poor one:

- It attempts to solve a general problem (or range of problems), rather than just performing a specific task
- It follows standard conventions that make it easier to use the module elsewhere
- The module is clearly documented so that other people can easily understand and use it

Let's take a closer look at each of these points.

Solving a general problem

Often when you are programming, you will find that you need a specific task performed, and so you write a function to perform this task. For example, consider the following:

- You need to convert from inches into centimeters, so you write an `inch_to_cm()` function to perform this task.

- You need to read a list of place names from a text file, which uses vertical bar characters (|) as delimiters between the fields:

  ```
  FEATURE_ID|FEATURE_NAME|FEATURE_CLASS|...
  1397658|Ester|Populated Place|...
  1397926|Afognak|Populated Place|...
  ```

  To do this, you create a `load_placenames()` function that reads data from this file.

- You need to display the number of customers to a user:

  ```
  1 customer
  8 customers
  ```

  Whether the message uses the word `customer` or `customers` depends on the number supplied. To handle this, you create a `pluralize_customers()` function that returns the appropriately pluralized version of the message depending on the number provided.

In all of these examples, you are solving a specific problem. Quite frequently, functions like this will end up as part of a module, which you may want to reuse or share with others. However, these three functions, `inch_to_cm()`, `load_placenames()`, and `pluralize_customers()`, are all very specific to the problem you were trying to solve and so have limited applicability to new programs. All three are crying out to be made more general:

- Instead of the `inch_to_cm()` function, write a function that converts *any* imperial distance into metric, and then create another function that does the opposite.

- Instead of writing a function that just loads place names, implement a `load_delimited_text()` function which works for any sort of delimited text file and doesn't assume particular column names or that the delimiter is a vertical bar character.

- Instead of pluralizing just customer names, write a more general `pluralize()` function that will pluralize the complete range of names you might need in your program. Because of the vagaries of the English language, you can't just assume that all names can be pluralized by adding an *s* to the end; you'll need a dictionary of exceptions such as person/people, axis/axes, and series/series, so that this function can handle the various sorts of names you might want to pluralize. To make this function even more useful, you can have it optionally accept the plural version of the name if it doesn't know about the type of units you are pluralizing:

```
def pluralize(n, singular_name, plural_name=None):
```

While these are just three specific examples, you can see that, by generalizing the code that you are sharing, you can make it apply to a much wider range of tasks. Often, there's very little more work involved in generalizing a function, but the result will be hugely appreciated by the people who use the code that you create.

Following standard conventions

While you can write code any way you like, if you want to share your code with others it makes sense to follow standard coding conventions. This makes it easier for others to use your code without having to remember your library's particular style.

To use a real-world example, consider the following snippet of code:

```
shapefile = ogr.Open("...")
layer = shapefile.GetLayer(0)
for i in range(layer.GetFeatureCount()):
  feature = layer.GetFeature(i)
  shape = shapely.loads(feature.GetGeometryRef().ExportToWkt())
  if shape.contains(target_zone):
    ...
```

This snippet of code makes use of two libraries: the Shapely library, which performs computational geometry, and the OGR library, which reads and writes geospatial data. The Shapely library follows the standard Python conventions of using lowercase letters for function and method names:

```
shapely.loads(...)
shape.contains(...)
```

While the details of these libraries are rather complex, the naming of these functions and methods is easy to remember and use. Compare this with the OGR library, however, which capitalizes the first letter of each function and method name:

```
ogr.Open(...)
layer.GetFeatureCount()
```

Using these two libraries together, you have to constantly remember that OGR capitalizes the first letter of each function and method name, while Shapely does not. This makes using OGR more awkward than it needs to be and leads to quite a few errors in the resulting code that then need to be fixed.

All of this could have been avoided if the OGR library had simply followed the same naming conventions as Shapely.

Fortunately, for Python there is a document called the **Python Style Guide** (`https://www.python.org/dev/peps/pep-0008/`) that provides a clear set of recommendations for how to format and style your code. The use of lowercase letters for function and method names comes from this guide, as does a whole raft of other recommendations which most Python code also follows. Everything from how to name your variables to when to place whitespace around a parenthesis is described in this document.

While coding conventions are a matter of personal preference, and you certainly aren't required to slavishly follow the instructions in the Python Style Guide, doing so (at least in so far as it affects the users of your code) will make your reusable modules and packages easier for others to use—just like with the example of the OGR library, you don't want users to have to constantly remember an unusual naming style whenever someone wants to import and use your code.

Having clear documentation

Even if you wrote the perfect module, solving a range of generalized problems and faithfully adhering to the Python Style Guide, your module would be useless if nobody knew how to use it. Unfortunately, as programmers, we are often too close to our code: it's obvious to us how our code works, and so we fall into the trap of assuming it must be obvious to others, too. On top of this, programmers often *hate* writing documentation—we'd much rather write a thousand lines of well-crafted Python code than one paragraph describing how it works. As a result, documentation for the code we share is often written reluctantly, if at all.

The thing is, a high-quality reusable module or package will *always* include documentation. This documentation will both explain what the module does and how it works, and include examples so that readers can immediately see how to use this module or package within their own programs.

For an example of an excellently documented Python module or package, we need look no further than the **Python Standard Library** (`https://docs.python.org/3/library/`). Every module is clearly documented, with detailed information and examples to help guide the programmer. For example, the following is an abbreviated version of the documentation for the `datetime.timedelta` class:

8.1.2. `timedelta` Objects

A `timedelta` object represents a duration, the difference between two dates or times.

class datetime.**timedelta**(*days=0, seconds=0, microseconds=0, milliseconds=0, minutes=0, hours=0, weeks=0*)

> All arguments are optional and default to 0. Arguments may be integers or floats, and may be positive or negative.

. . .

Supported operations:

Operation	Result
t1 = t2 + t3	Sum of *t2* and *t3*. Afterwards *t1-t2* == *t3* and *t1-t3* == *t2* are true. (1)
t1 = t2 - t3	Difference of *t2* and *t3*. Afterwards *t1* == *t2 - t3* and *t2* == *t1 + t3* are true. (1)

. . .

Example usage:

```
>>> from datetime import timedelta
>>> year = timedelta(days=365)
>>> another_year = timedelta(weeks=40, days=84, hours=23,
...                          minutes=50, seconds=600)  # adds up to 365 days
>>> year.total_seconds()
31536000.0
```

Every module, class, function, and method is clearly documented, with examples and detailed notes to help the user of this module.

As the developer of a reusable module, you aren't expected to quite reach these heights. The Python Standard Library is a huge, collaborative effort, and no one person wrote all this documentation. But this is a good example of the *type* of documentation that you should be aiming for: comprehensive documentation with plenty of examples.

While you can create documentation in a word processor, or using a sophisticated documentation-generation system such as the Sphinx system used to build the Python documentation, there are two very easy ways in which you can write documentation with a minimum of fuss: by creating a README file, or by using docstrings.

A README file is simply a text file that gets included with the various source files which make up your module or package. It would typically be named README.txt, and it is just an ordinary text file. You can create this file using the same editor that you use to edit your Python source code.

A README file can be as extensive or minimal as you want. It is often helpful to include information on how to install and use the module, any licensing issues, a few usage examples, and acknowledgements if your module or package includes code from someone else.

A docstring is a Python string that gets *attached* to a module or function. This is used specifically for documentation purposes, and there is a very special Python syntax for creating docstrings:

```
""" my_module.py

    This is the documentation for the my_module module.
"""
def my_function():
    """ This is the documentation for the my_function() function.

        As you can see, the documentation can span more than
        one line.
    """
    ...
```

In Python, you can use three quote characters to mark a string that goes across more than one line of the Python source file. These triple-quoted strings can be used in various places, including docstrings. If a module starts with a triple-quoted string, then this string is used as the documentation for the module as a whole. Similarly, if any function starts with a triple-quoted string, then this string is used as documentation for that function.

 The same applies to other definitions in Python, such as classes, methods, and so on.

Docstrings are typically used to describe what a module or function does, the parameters that are needed, and what information is returned. Any noteworthy aspects of the module or function should also be included, for example unexpected side effects, usage examples, and so on.

Docstrings (and README files) don't have to be very extensive. You don't want to spend hours writing documentation on some obscure function within a module that only three people are ever likely to use. But well-written docstrings and README files are a sign of an excellent and easy-to-use module or package.

Writing documentation is a skill; like all skills, you get better at it with practice. To create high-quality modules and packages that can be shared, you should get into the habit of creating docstrings and README files as well as following coding conventions and generalizing your code as much as possible, as we described in previous sections of this chapter. If you aim to produce high-quality reusable code from the outset, you'll find that it isn't that hard.

Examples of reusable modules

You don't have to look very far to find examples of reusable modules; the **Python Package Index** (`https://pypi.python.org/pypi`) provides a huge repository of shared modules and packages. You can search for a package by name or keyword, or you can browse through the repository by topic, license, intended audience, development status, and so on.

While the Python Package Index is huge, it is also extremely useful: all of the most successful packages and modules are included. Let's look more closely at some of these more popular reusable packages.

requests

The `requests` library (`http://docs.python-requests.org/en/master/`) is a Python package that makes it easy to send HTTP requests to remote servers and process the response. While the `urllib2` package included in the Python Standard Library does allow you to make HTTP requests, it is often difficult to use and fails in unexpected ways. The `requests` package is far easier to use and more reliable; as a result, it has become extremely popular.

The following example code shows how the `requests` library allows you to send a complex HTTP request and easily process the response:

```
import requests

response = requests.post("http://server.com/api/login",
                         {'username' : username,
                          'password' : password})
if response.status_code == 200: # OK
    user = response.json()
    if user['logged_in']:
        ...
```

The `requests` library automatically encodes the parameters that you want to send to the server, gracefully handles timeouts, and makes it easy to retrieve a JSON-format response.

The requests library is very easy to install (in most cases, you can simply use pip install requests). It has excellent documentation, including a user's guide, a community guide, and detailed API documentation, and it fully conforms with the Python Style Guide. It also provides a very general set of features, handling all sorts of communication with external web sites and systems via the HTTP protocol. With all these things going for it, it's no wonder that `requests` is the third most popular package in the entire Python Package Index.

python-dateutil

The `dateutil` package (`https://github.com/dateutil/dateutil`) extends the `datetime` package included in the Python Standard Library, adding support for recurring dates, time zones, complex relative dates, and more.

The following example code calculates the date of Easter Friday in a much easier form than we used for the *happy hour* calculation in the previous chapter:

```
from dateutil.easter import easter
easter_friday = easter(today.year) - datetime.timedelta(days=2)
```

`dateutil` provides excellent documentation with plenty of examples, is easy to install using `pip install python-dateutil`, follows the Python Style guide, and is extremely useful for solving a range of date- and time-related challenges. It is another example of a successful and popular package within the Python Package Index.

lxml

The lxml toolkit (http://lxml.de) is an example of a highly successful Python package that acts as a wrapper for two existing C libraries. As the well-written web site says, lxml takes the pain out of reading and writing XML- and HTML-formatted documents. It has been modeled after an existing library in the Python Standard Library (ElementTree) but is much faster, has more features, and won't crash in unexpected ways.

The following example code shows how lxml can be used to quickly generate XML-format data:

```
from lxml import etree

movies = etree.Element("movie")
movie = etree.SubElement(movies, "movie")
movie.text = "The Wizard of Oz"
movie.set("year", "1939")

movie = etree.SubElement(movies, "movie")
movie.text = "Mary Poppins"
movie.set("year", "1964")

movie = etree.SubElement(movies, "movie")
movie.text = "Chinatown"
movie.set("year", "1974")

print(etree.tostring(movies, pretty_print=True))
```

This will print out an XML-formatted document with information about three classic movies:

```
<movie>
  <movie year="1939">The Wizard of Oz</movie>
  <movie year="1964">Mary Poppins</movie>
  <movie year="1974">Chinatown</movie>
</movie>
```

Of course, lxml can do much more than this simple example shows. It can be used to parse documents as well as programmatically generate huge and complex XML files.

The lxml web site includes excellent documentation, including tutorials, information on how to install the package, and a complete API reference. For the particular tasks that it solves, lxml is extremely inviting and easy to use. It is no wonder that this is a highly popular package within the Python Package Index.

Designing a reusable package

Let's now take what we've learned and apply it to the design and implementation of a useful Python package. In the previous chapter, we looked at the concept of encapsulating a recipe using a Python module. Part of each recipe is the notion of an ingredient, which has three parts:

- The name of the ingredient
- How much of the ingredient is needed
- The units in which the ingredient is measured

If we want to work with ingredients, we need to be able to handle units properly. For example, adding 1.5 kilograms to 750 grams involves more than adding the numbers 1.5 and 750—you have to know how to *convert* these values from one unit to another.

In the case of recipes, there are a number of rather unusual conversions that you need to support. For example, did you know that three teaspoons of sugar equals one tablespoon of sugar? To handle these types of conversions, let's write a unit conversion library.

Our unit converter will have to be aware of all the standard units used in cooking. These include cups, tablespoons, teaspoons, grams, ounces, pounds, and so on. Our unit converter will need some way of representing a quantity, such as 1.5 kilograms, and of converting quantities from one unit to another.

As well as representing and converting quantities, we would like our library to be able to display quantities, automatically using the singular or plural version of the unit name as appropriate, for example, **6 cups**, **1 gallon**, **150 grams**, and so on.

Since we're displaying quantities, it would also be helpful if our library could parse quantities. This way, the user could enter a value such as 3 tbsp and our library would know that the user entered a quantity of three tablespoons.

The more we think about this library, the more it seems like a useful tool in its own right. We thought of this in connection with our recipe-handling program, but it seems that this could be an ideal candidate for a reusable module or package.

Following the guidelines we looked at earlier, let's consider how we can generalize our library as much as possible to make it more useful in other programs and to other programmers.

Rather than just thinking about the sorts of quantities you might find in a recipe, let's change the scope of our library to handle *any* type of quantity. It could handle weights, lengths, areas, volumes, and possibly even units of time, force, speed, and the like.

Thinking of it like this, our library isn't so much a unit converter as a library that works with **quantities**. A quantity is a number and its associated units, for example, 150 millimeters, 1.5 ounces, or 5 acres. Our library, which we will call Quantities, will be a tool for parsing, displaying, and creating quantities, as well as converting quantities from one unit to another. As you can see, our initial concept for the library is now just one of the things that the library will be able to do.

Let's now design our Quantities library in more detail. We'd like the user of our library to be able to create a new quantity very easily. For example:

```
q = quantities.new(5, "kilograms")
```

We also want to be able to parse a string into a quantity value, like this:

```
q = quantities.parse("3 tbsp")
```

We then want to be able to display a quantity in the following manner:

```
print(q)
```

We also want to be able to tell what kind of value a quantity is representing, for example:

```
>>> print(quantities.kind(q))
weight
```

This will let us tell whether a quantity represents a weight, a length, or a distance, among others.

We can also retrieve the value and units for a quantity:

```
>>> print(quantities.value(q))
3
>>> print(quantities.units(q))
tablespoon
```

We also need the ability to convert a quantity into a different unit. For example:

```
>>> q = quantities.new(2.5, "cups")
>>> print(quantities.convert(q, "liter"))
0.59147059125 liters
```

Finally, we would like to be able to get a list of all the kinds of units that our library supports and the individual units of each kind:

```
>>> for kind in quantities.supported_kinds():
>>>     for unit in quantities.supported_units(kind):
```

```
>>>            print(kind, unit)
weight gram
weight kilogram
weight ounce
weight pound
length millimeter
...
```

There is one final feature that our Quantities library will need to support: the ability to *localize* units and quantities. Unfortunately, the conversion values for certain quantities will vary depending on whether you are in the United States or elsewhere. For example, in the U.S. a teaspoon has a volume of approximately 4.93 cubic centimeters, while in the rest of the world a teaspoon is considered to have a volume of 5 cubic centimeters. There are also naming conventions to deal with: in the U.S. the base unit of length in the metric system is referred to as a *meter*, while in the rest of the world the same unit is spelled *metre*. Our unit will have to handle both the different conversion values and the different naming conventions.

To do this, we will need to support the notion of a **locale**. When our library is initialized, the caller will specify the locale under which our module should operate:

```
quantities.init("international")
```

This will affect the conversion values and spelling used by the library:

Given the complexity of our Quantities library, it doesn't make sense to try and squeeze all this into a single module. Instead, we'll break our library up into three separate modules: a `units` module which defines all the different type of units that we support, an `interface` module which implements the various public functions for our package, and a `quantity` module which encapsulates the concept of a quantity being a value and its associated unit.

These three modules will be combined into a single Python package, which we will call `quantities`.

> Note that we deliberately used the term *library* to refer to the system as we were designing it; this ensured that we didn't pre-empt our design by thinking of it as a single module or as a package. Only now is it clear that we are going to write a Python package. Often, something that you think of as a module will end up growing into a package. Occasionally the opposite happens. It's important to be flexible about this.

Now that we have a good design for our Quantities library, what it will do, and how we'd like to structure it, let's start writing some code.

Implementing a reusable package

 This section includes a lot of source code. Remember that you don't have to type it all in by hand; a complete copy of the `quantities` package is provided as part of the sample code that can be downloaded for this chapter.

Start by creating the directory named `quantities` to hold our new package. Inside this directory, create a new file named `quantity.py`. This module will hold our implementation of a quantity — that is, a value together with its associated units.

While you don't need to understand object-oriented programming techniques to work through this book, this is the one place where we need to use object-oriented programming. This is because we want the user to be able to print a quantity directly, and the only way to do that in Python is to use objects. Don't worry, though — this code is very straightforward, and we'll take it one step at a time.

In the `quantity.py` module, enter the following Python code:

```
class Quantity(object):
    def __init__(self, value, units):
        self.value = value
        self.units = units
```

What we are doing here is defining a new type of object called a `Quantity`. The second line looks very much like a function definition, only we are defining a special type of function, called a **method**, and giving it a special name, `__init__`. This method is used to initialize a new object when it is created. The `self` parameter refers to the object that is being created; as you can see, our `__init__` function takes two additional parameters named `value` and `units`, and stores these two values into `self.value` and `self.units`.

With our new `Quantity` object defined, we can create new objects and retrieve their values. For example:

```
q = Quantity(1, "inch")
print(q.value, q.units)
```

The first line creates a new object using the Quantity class, passing 1 for the value parameter and "inch" for the units parameter. The __init__ method then stores these within the value and units attributes within the object. As you can see in the second line, it's easy to retrieve these attributes when we need them.

We've almost completed our implementation of the quantity.py module. There's just one more thing to do: in order to be able to print a Quantity value, we need to add another method to our Quantity class; this one will be called __str__ and will be used whenever we need to print a quantity. To do this, add the following Python code to the end of your quantity.py module:

```python
def __str__(self):
    return "{} {}".format(self.value, self.units)
```

Make sure that the def statement is indented to the same level as the def __init__() statement earlier so that it's part of the class we're creating. This will allow us to do things such as the following:

```python
>>> q = Quantity(1, "inch")
>>> print(q)
1 inch
```

The Python print() function calls the specially named __str__ method to get the text to display for a quantity. Our __str__ method returns the value and the units, separated by a single space, which makes for a nicely formatted summary of the quantity.

This completes our quantity.py module. As you can see, working with objects wasn't as difficult as it might seem.

Our next task is to collect all the information we need to store about the various units that our package will support. Because there is a lot of information here, we'll put this into a module by itself, which we will call units.py.

Create the units.py module within your quantities package, and start by entering the following into this file:

```python
UNITS = {}
```

The UNITS dictionary will map the kind of unit to a list of the units defined for that kind. For example, all units of length would go into the UNITS['length'] list.

For each unit, we will store the information about that unit in the form of a dictionary with the following entries:

Dictionary entry	Description
`name`	The name for this unit, for example, `inch`.
`abbreviation`	The official abbreviation for this unit, for example, `in`.
`plural`	The plural name for this unit. This is the name to use when there is more than one of this unit, for example, `inches`.
`num_units`	The number of units needed to convert between these units and others of the same type. For example, if the `centimeter` unit had a `num_units` value of `1`, then the `inch` unit would have a `num_units` value of `2.54` because 1 inch equals 2.54 centimeters.

As we discussed in the previous section, we need to be able to localize our various units and quantities. To allow for this, all of these dictionary entries can either have a single value or a dictionary mapping each locale to a value. For example, the `liter` unit might be defined using the following Python dictionary:

```
{'name' : {'us'              : "liter",
           'international' : "litre"},
 'plural' : {'us'            : "liters",
             'international' : "litres"},
 'abbreviation' : "l",
 'num_units' : 1000}
```

This allows us to have a different spelling for the word `liter` in different locales. Other units might have different numbers of units or different abbreviations, depending on the locale selected.

Now that we know how we're going to store our various unit definitions, let's implement the next part of our `units.py` module. To avoid having to repetitively type lots of unit dictionaries, we're going to create a few helper functions. Add the following to the end of your module:

```
def by_locale(value_for_us, value_for_international):
    return {"us"              : value_for_us,
            "international" : value_for_international}
```

This function will return a dictionary mapping the `us` and `international` locales to the given values, making it easier to create a locale-specific dictionary entry.

Next, add the following function to your module:

```
def unit(*args):
    if len(args) == 3:
        abbreviation = args[0]
        name         = args[1]

        if isinstance(name, dict):
            plural = {}
            for key,value in name.items():
                plural[key] = value + "s"
        else:
            plural = name + "s"

        num_units = args[2]
    elif len(args) == 4:
        abbreviation = args[0]
        name         = args[1]
        plural       = args[2]
        num_units    = args[3]
    else:
        raise RuntimeError("Bad arguments to unit(): {}".format(args))

    return {'abbreviation' : abbreviation,
            'name'         : name,
            'plural'       : plural,
            'num_units'    : num_units}
```

This complex-looking function creates the dictionary entry for a single unit. It uses the special `*args` parameter form to accept a variable number of parameters; the caller can provide either an abbreviation, a name, and the number of units, or else the abbreviation, the name, the plural name, and the number of units. If the plural name is not provided, it is calculated automatically by adding s to the end of the unit's singular name.

Note that the logic here allows for the possibility of the name being a dictionary of locale-specific names; if the name is localized, then the plural name will also be calculated on a locale-by-locale basis.

Finally, we define a simple helper function that makes it easier to define a list of units all at once:

```
def units(kind, *units_to_add):
    if kind not in UNITS:
        UNITS[kind] = []

    for unit in units_to_add:
        UNITS[kind].append(unit)
```

With all these helper functions in place, it will be quite easy for us to add our various units to the UNITS dictionary. Add the following code to the end of your module; this defines the various weight-based units that our package will support:

```
units("weight",
    unit("g",  "gram",     1),
    unit("kg", "kilogram", 1000))
    unit("oz", "ounce",    28.349523125),
    unit("lb", "pound",    453.59237))
```

Next, add some length-based units:

```
units("length",
    unit("cm", by_locale("centimeter", "centimetre"), 1),
    unit("m",  by_locale("meter",      "metre",       100),
    unit("in", "inch", "inches", 2.54)
    unit("ft", "foot", "feet", 30.48))
```

As you can see, we've use the by_locale() function to create different versions of the unit name and plural name based on the user's current locale. We also supply the plural name for the inch and foot units as these can't be calculated by adding an s to the singular version of the name.

Let's now add some area-based units:

```
units("area",
    unit("sq m", by_locale("square meter", "square metre"), 1),
    unit("ha",    "hectare", 10000),
    unit("a",     "acre",    4046.8564224))
```

Finally, we'll define some volume-based units:

```
units("volume",
    unit("l",  by_locale("liter", "litre"), 1000),
    unit("ml", by_locale("milliliter", "millilitre"), 1),
    unit("c",  "cup", localize(236.5882365, 250)))
```

For the "cup" unit, we are localizing the number of units rather than the name. This is because in the US a cup is considered to be 236.588 mls, while elsewhere in the world a cup is measured as 250 mls.

 These unit listings have been abbreviated to keep the code listing to a reasonable size. The version of the quantities package included in the sample code for this chapter has a more comprehensive list of units.

This completes our unit definitions. To make it easy for our code to use these various units, we're going to add two extra functions to the end of our units.py module. First off is a function to choose the appropriate localized version of a value from a unit's dictionary:

```
def localize(value, locale):
    if isinstance(value, dict):
        return value.get(locale)
    else:
        return value
```

As you can see, we check to see if value is a dictionary; if so, we return the entry within that dictionary for the supplied locale. Otherwise, we return value directly. We'll use this function whenever we need to retrieve a name, plural name, abbreviation, or value from a unit's dictionary.

The second function we are going to need is a function to search through the various units stored in the UNITS global variable. We want to be able to find a unit based on its singular or plural name, or its abbreviation, allowing for the spelling specific to the current locale. To do this, add the following code to the end of the units.py module:

```
def find_unit(s, locale):
    s = s.lower()
    for kind in UNITS.keys():
        for unit in UNITS[kind]:
            if (s == localize(unit['abbreviation'],
                              locale).lower() or
                s == localize(unit['name'],
                              locale).lower() or
                s == localize(unit['plural'],
                              locale).lower()):
                # Success!
                return (kind, unit)

    return (None, None) # Not found.
```

Notice that we use `s.lower()` to convert the string to lowercase before checking it. This ensures that we find the `inch` unit, for example, even if the user spelled it as `Inch` or `INCH`. Upon completion, our `find_units()` function returns the kind of unit and the unit dictionary for the found unit, or `(None, None)` if the unit can't be found.

This completes the `units.py` module. Let's now create the `interface.py` module, which will hold the public interface to our `quantities` package.

> We could put all this code directly in the package initialization file,
> `__init__.py`, but this can be a bit confusing as many programmers
> don't expect to find code within an `__init__.py` file. Instead, we'll
> define all our public functions in the `interface.py` module, and
> import the contents of this module into `__init__.py`.

Create the `interface.py` module, placing it into the `quantities` package directory alongside `units.py` and `quantities.py`. Then, add the following `import` statements to the top of this module:

```
from .units import UNITS, localize, find_unit
from .quantity import Quantity
```

As you can see, we are using a relative import statement to load the `UNITS` global variable and the `localize()` and `find_unit()` functions from our `units.py` module. We then use another relative import to load the `Quantity` class which we defined in our `quantity.py` module. This makes these important functions, classes, and variables available for our code to use.

We now need to implement the various functions we identified in the previous section of this chapter. We'll start with `init()`, which initializes the entire quantities package. Add the following to the end of your `interface.py` module:

```
def init(locale):
    global _locale
    _locale = locale
```

The caller will provide the name of a locale (which should be a string containing either `us` or `international` as these are the two locales we are supporting), which we store into a private global variable named `_locale`.

The next function we want to implement is `new()`. This lets the user define a new quantity by supplying a value and the name of the desired units. We'll use the `find_unit()` function to make sure the unit exists, and then create and return a new `Quantity` object with the supplied value and units:

```
def new(value, units):
    global _locale
    kind,unit = find_unit(units, _locale)
    if kind == None:
        raise ValueError("Unknown unit: {}".format(units))

    return Quantity(value, localize(unit['name'], _locale))
```

Because the name of the unit can vary depending on the locale, we use the `_locale` private global variable to help find the unit with the supplied name, plural name, or abbreviation. Once a unit has been found, we use the official name of that unit to create a new `Quantity` object, which we then return to the caller.

As well as creating a new quantity by supplying the value and units, we also need to implement a `parse()` function that converts a string into a `Quantity` object. Let's do this now:

```
def parse(s):
    global _locale

    sValue,sUnits = s.split(" ", maxsplit=1)
    value = float(sValue)

    kind,unit = find_unit(sUnits, _locale)
    if kind == None:
        raise ValueError("Unknown unit: {}".format(sUnits))

    return Quantity(value, localize(unit['name'], _locale))
```

We split the string at the first space, converting the first part into a floating-point number and searching for a unit with a name or abbreviation equal to the second part of the string.

Next up, we need to write some functions to return information about a quantity. Let's just go ahead and implement these functions by adding the following code to the end of your `interface.py` module:

```
def kind(q):
    global _locale
    kind,unit = find_unit(q.units, _locale)
```

```
        return kind

def value(q):
    return q.value

def units(q):
    return q.units
```

These functions allow the user of our package to identify the kind of units associated with a given quantity (for example, length, weight, or volume), and to retrieve a quantity's value and units.

> Note that the user could also retrieve these last two values by accessing the attributes within the Quantity object directly, for example, print(q.value). We can't stop the user from doing this but, because we're not implementing this as an object-oriented package, we don't want to encourage it.

We are almost there. Our next function will convert a quantity from one unit to another, returning a ValueError if the conversion is impossible. Here is the necessary code to do this:

```
def convert(q, units):
    global _locale

    src_kind,src_units = find_unit(q.units, _locale)
    dst_kind,dst_units = find_unit(units, _locale)

    if src_kind == None:
        raise ValueError("Unknown units: {}".format(q.units))
    if dst_kind == None:
        raise ValueError("Unknown units: {}".format(units))

    if src_kind != dst_kind:
        raise ValueError(
                "It's impossible to convert {} into {}!".format(
                        localize(src_units['plural'], _locale),
                        localize(dst_units['plural'], _locale)))

    num_units = (q.value * src_units['num_units'] /
                dst_units['num_units'])
    return Quantity(num_units, localize(dst_units['name'],
                                        _locale))
```

The final two functions we need to implement return a list of the different kinds of unit we support and a list of the individual units of a given kind. Here are the final two functions for our `interface.py` module:

```
def supported_kinds():
    return list(UNITS.keys())

def supported_units(kind):
    global _locale

    units = []
    for unit in UNITS.get(kind, []):
        units.append(localize(unit['name'], _locale))
    return units
```

Now that we've finished implementing the `interface.py` module, there is only one last thing to do: create the package initialization file for our `quantities` package, `__init__.py`, and enter the following into this file:

```
from .interface import *
```

This makes all of the functions we defined in the `interface.py` module available to users of our package.

Testing our reusable package

Now that we've written the code (or alternatively, downloaded it), let's take a look at how this package works. In a terminal window, set the current directory to the folder containing your `quantities` package directory, and type `python` to start the Python interpreter. Then, type the following:

```
>>> import quantities
```

If you haven't made any mistakes in typing in the source code, the interpreter should come back without any errors. If you have made any typos, you'll need to fix them before you can proceed.

Next, we have to initialize our `quantities` package by supplying the locale we want to use:

```
>>> quantities.init("international")
```

If you are in the United States, feel free to replace the value `international` with `us` so that you get localized spelling and units for your country.

Let's create a simple quantity, and then ask the Python interpreter to display it:

```
>>> q = quantities.new(24, "km")
>>>> print(q)
24 kilometre
```

As you can see, the international spelling for the word `kilometer` is automatically used.

Let's try converting this unit into inches:

```
>>> print(quantities.convert(q, "inch"))
944881.8897637795 inch
```

There are other functions we haven't tested yet, but already we can see that our `quantities` package solves a very general problem, conforms to the Python Style guide, and is easy to use. It isn't quite an ideal reusable module, but it's close. Here are a few things we could do to improve it:

- Restructure our package to be more object-oriented. For example, instead of calling `quantities.convert(q, "inch")`, users could simply say `q.convert("inch")`.

- Improve the implementation of the `__str__()` function so that the unit name is displayed as a plural if the value is greater than one. Also, change the code to avoid floating-point rounding issues, which can produce odd results when printing out certain quantity values.

- Add functions (or methods) to add, subtract, multiply, and divide quantities.

- Add docstrings to our package source code, and then use a tool such as **Sphinx** (`http://www.sphinx-doc.org`) to convert the docstrings into API documentation for our package.

- Upload the source code for the `quantities` package to **GitHub** (`https://github.com`) to make it easier to obtain.

- Create a web site (possibly as a simple README file within the GitHub repository) so that people can find out more about this package.

- Submit the package to the PyPI so that people can find it.

Feel free to extend the `quantities` package and submit it if you want; this is only an example for this book, but it certainly has potential as a general-purpose (and popular) reusable Python package.

Summary

In this chapter, we looked at the concept of a reusable module or package. We saw how reusable packages and modules can be used to share code with other people. We learned that a reusable module or package needs to function as a standalone unit, should ideally use relative imports, and should note any external dependencies it may have. Ideally, a reusable package or module will also solve a general problem rather than a specific one, follow standard Python coding conventions, and have good documentation. We then looked at some examples of good reusable modules, before writing one of our own.

In the next chapter, we will look at some of the more advanced aspects of working with modules and packages in Python.

7
Advanced Module Techniques

In this chapter, we will look at a number of more advanced techniques for working with modules and packages. In particular, we will:

- Examine the more unusual ways in which the `import` statement can be used, including optional imports, local imports, and how to tweak the way importing works by changing `sys.path`
- Briefly examine a number of "gotchas" relating to importing modules and packages
- Take a look at how you can use the Python interactive interpreter to help develop your modules and packages more quickly
- Learn how to work with global variables within a module or package
- See how to configure a package
- Discover how to include data files as part of your Python package.

Optional imports

Try opening the Python interactive interpreter and entering the following command:

```
import nonexistent_module
```

The interpreter will return the following error message:

```
ImportError: No module named 'nonexistent_module'
```

This shouldn't be a surprise to you; you may have even seen this error in your own programs if you made a typo within an `import` statement.

The interesting thing about this error is that it doesn't just apply where you've made a typo. You can also use this to test if a module or package is available on this particular computer, for example:

```
try:
    import numpy
    has_numpy = True
except ImportError:
    has_numpy = False
```

You can then use this to have your program take advantage of the module if it is present, or do something else if the module or package isn't available, like this:

```
if has_numpy:
    array = numpy.zeros((num_rows, num_cols), dtype=numpy.int32)
else:
    array = []
    for row in num_rows:
        array.append([])
```

In this example, we check to see if the numpy library was installed, and if so, use numpy.zeros() to create a two-dimensional array. Otherwise, we use a list of lists instead. This allows your program to take advantage of the speed of the NumPy library if it was installed, while still working (albeit more slowly) if this library isn't available.

 Note that this example is just made up; you probably wouldn't be able to use a list of lists directly instead of a NumPy array and have the rest of your program work without any change. But the concept of doing one thing if a module is present, and something else if it is not, remains the same.

Using optional imports like this is a great way of having your module or package take advantage of other libraries, while still working if they aren't installed. Of course, you should always mention these optional imports in the documentation for your package so that your users will know what will happen if these optional modules or packages are installed.

Local imports

In *Chapter 3*, *Using Modules and Packages*, we introduced the concept of a **global namespace**, and showed how the `import` statement adds the name of the imported module or package into the global namespace. This description was actually a slight oversimplification. In fact, the `import` statement adds the imported module or package to the *current* namespace, which may or may not be the global namespace.

In Python, there are two namespaces: the global namespace and the local namespace. The global namespace is where all the top-level definitions in your source file are stored. For example, consider the following Python module:

```python
import random
import string

def set_length(lcngth):
    global _length
    _length = length

def make_name():
    global _length

    letters = []
    for i in range(length):
        letters.append(random.choice(string.letters))
    return "".join(letters)
```

When you import this Python module, you will have added four entries to the global namespace: `random`, `string`, `set_length`, and `make_name`.

 There are several other entries in the global namespace, automatically added by the Python interpreter. We'll ignore these for now.

If you then call the `set_length()` function, the `global` statement at the top of this function will add another entry to the module's global namespace, called `_length`. The `make_name()` function also includes a `global` statement, allowing it to refer to the global `_length` value while generating a random name.

So far so good. The thing that may not be so obvious is that, within each function, there is a second namespace called the **local namespace**, that holds all variables and other definitions that aren't global. In the `make_name()` function, the `letters` list, as well as the variable `i` used by the `for` statement, are *local* variables—they only exist within the local namespace, and their values are lost when the function exits.

The local namespace isn't just for local variables: you can use it for local imports, too. For example, consider the following function:

```
def delete_backups(dir):
    import os
    import os.path
    for filename in os.listdir(dir):
        if filename.endswith(".bak"):
            remove(os.path.join(dir, filename))
```

Notice how the os and os.path modules are imported *within* the function, rather than at the top of a module or other source file. Because these modules are imported within the function, the os and os.path names are added to the local namespace rather than the global namespace.

In most cases, you should avoid using local imports: having all your import statements near the top of the source file (and so making all your import statements global) makes it easier to see at a glance which modules your source file depends upon. There are, however, two situations where local imports can be useful:

1. If the module or package you are importing is particularly large or is slow to initialize itself, your module will be quicker to import if you use a local import rather than a global one. The delay when importing the module will only show up when your function is called. This can be particularly useful if the function is only called in certain circumstances.

2. Local imports are a great way of avoiding circular dependencies. If module A depends on module B and module B depends on module A, then your program will crash if both sets of imports are global. However, changing one set of imports to be a local import will break the co-dependency since the import won't take place until your function is called.

As a general rule you should stick to global imports, though local imports can be very useful in these special situations.

Tweaking imports using sys.path

When you use the import command, the Python interpreter has to search for the module or package you want to import. It does this by looking through the **module search path**, which is a list of the various directories where modules or packages can be found. The module search path is stored in sys.path, and the Python interpreter will check the directories in this list one after another until the desired module or package is found.

When the Python interpreter starts, it initializes the module search path with the following directories:

- The directory containing the currently-executing script, or the current directory if you are running the Python interactive interpreter in a terminal window

- Any directories listed in the PYTHONPATH environment variable

- The contents of the interpreter's site-packages directory, including any modules referred to by path configuration files within the site-packages directory

 The site-packages directory is used to hold the various third-party modules and packages that you install. For example, if you use the Python Package Manager, pip, to install a Python module or package, that module or package would normally be placed within the site-packages directory.

- A number of directories containing the various modules and packages that make up the Python Standard Library

The order in which these directories appear in sys.path is important because the search stops as soon as a module or package with the desired name is found.

You can print out the contents of your module search path if you wish, though the list is likely to be long and rather hard to understand as there are often many directories containing the various parts of the Python Standard Library as well as other directories used by any third-party packages you may have installed:

```
>>> import sys
>>> print(sys.path)
['', '/usr/local/lib/python3.3/site-packages', '/Library/Frameworks/
SQLite3.framework/Versions/B/Python/3.3', '/Library/Python/3.3/site-
packages/numpy-override', '/Library/Python/3.3/site-packages/pip-1.5.6-
py3.3.egg', '/usr/local/lib/python3.3.zip', '/usr/local/lib/python3.3',
'/usr/local/lib/python3.3/plat-darwin', '/usr/local/lib/python3.3/
lib-dynload', '/Library/Frameworks/Python.framework/Versions/3.3/lib/
python3.3', '/Library/Frameworks/Python.framework/Versions/3.3/lib/
python3.3/plat-darwin']
```

The important thing to remember is that this list is searched *in sequence* until a match is found. As soon as a module or package is found with the desired name, the search stops.

Now, sys.path is not just a read-only list. If you alter this list, for example by adding a new directory, you will change the places where the Python interpreter searches for modules.

There are actually a few modules that are built in to the Python interpreter; these are always imported directly, ignoring the module search path. To see which modules have been built in to your Python interpreter, you can execute the following commands:

```
import sys
print(sys.builtin_module_names)
```

If you try to import one of these modules, the built-in version will always be used, regardless of what you do to the module search path.

While you can make any changes you like to sys.path, for instance by removing or rearranging the contents of this list, the most common use is to add entries to the list. For example, you might want to store the various modules and packages that you create in a special directory, which you can then access from any Python program that needs it. For example, imagine that you have a directory at /usr/local/shared-python-libs which contains several modules and packages you've written that you want to use within a number of different Python programs. Within that directory, imagine that you have a module named utils.py and a package named approxnums that you wish to use in your program. While a simple import utils would fail with an ImportError, you can make the contents of your shared-python-libs directory available to your program in the following manner:

```
import sys
sys.path.append("/usr/local/shared-python-libs")
import utils, approxnums
```

You might be wondering why you can't just store your shared modules and packages within the site-packages directory. There are two reasons for this: first, because the site-packages directory is often protected and can only be written to by an administrator, which makes it hard to create and modify files stored in this directory. The second reason is that you might want to keep your own shared modules separate from other third-party modules that you've installed.

In the previous example, we modified `sys.path` by appending our `shared-python-libs` directory to the end of this list. While this works, remember that the module search path is searched *in sequence*. If there was any other module in any directory on the module search path named `utils.py`, that module would be imported rather than the one in your `shared-python-libs` directory. For this reason, rather than appending, you would normally modify `sys.path` in the following way:

```
sys.path.insert(1, "/usr/local/shared-python-libs")
```

Notice that we use `insert(1, ...)` rather than `insert(0, ...)`. This has the effect of adding the new directory as the *second* entry in `sys.path`. Since the first entry in the module search path is normally the directory containing the currently executing script, adding the new directory as the second entry means that the program's directory will be searched first. This helps to avoid confusing errors where you define a module within your program's directory and find that a different module with the same name is being imported instead. For this reason, it is good practice to use `insert(1, ...)` when adding a directory to `sys.path`.

Note that, like any other technique, modifying `sys.path` can be abused. If your reusable module or package modifies `sys.path`, users of your code may be confused by subtle bugs that show up because you've changed the module search path. As a general rule, you should only ever change the module search path in a main program rather than a reusable module and always clearly document what you've done so that there are no surprises.

Import gotchas

While modules and packages are extremely useful, there are times when Python's `import` machinery can leave you with subtle problems that can take a long time to figure out. In this section, we will discuss some of the more common problems that you are likely to encounter while working with modules and packages.

Using an existing name for your module or package

Imagine that you're writing a program that makes use of the Python Standard Library. For example, you might make use of the `random` module to do the following:

```
import random
print(random.choice(["yes", "no"]))
```

Your program is working correctly until you decide that it has too many mathematical functions in the main script, and you refactor it to move these functions into a separate module. You decide to call this module `math.py`, and store it in your main program's directory. As soon as you do this, the previous code will crash with the following error:

```
Traceback (most recent call last):
  File "main.py", line 5, in <module>
    import random
  File "/Library/Frameworks/Python.framework/Versions/3.3/lib/python3.3/
random.py", line 41, in <module>
    from math import log as _log, exp as _exp, pi as _pi, e as _e, ceil
as _ceil
ImportError: cannot import name log
```

What on earth is going on here? Code that was working perfectly now crashes, even though you haven't changed it. To make matters worse, the traceback shows that it's crashing at the point where your program imports a module from the Python Standard Library!

To understand what is going on here, you need to remember that the module search path by default includes the current program's directory as the first entry—ahead of other entries which point to the various parts of the Python Standard Library. By creating a new module named `math.py` as part of your program, you've made it impossible for the Python interpreter to load the `math.py` module from the Python Standard Library. This applies not just to the code you write but to *any* module or package on the module search path that may try to load this module from the Python Standard Library. In this example, it was the `random` module that failed, but it could have been any module that depended on the `math` library.

This is known as **name masking,** and is a particularly insidious problem. To avoid it, you should always be careful when choosing the names for the top-level modules and packages in your program to make sure they don't mask a module in the Python Standard Library, regardless of whether you use that module or not.

An easy way to avoid name masking is to make use of a package to organize the modules and packages you write within your program. For example, you might create a top-level package named `lib`, and create your various modules and packages within the `lib` package. Since there's no module or package named `lib` in the Python Standard Library, there's no risk of you masking a Standard Library module, no matter what name you choose for the modules and packages you place inside the `lib` package.

Naming a Python script after a module or package

A more subtle example of name masking can occur when you have a Python script that has the same name as a module in the Python Standard Library. For example, imagine that you're trying to figure out how the re module (https://docs.python.org/3.3/library/re.html) works. This module can be a bit confusing if you haven't worked with regular expressions before, so you might decide to write a simple test script to discover how it works. This test script might include the following code:

```
import re

pattern = input("Regular Expression: ")
s = input("String: ")

results = re.search(pattern, s)

print(results.group(), results.span())
```

This program might help you to figure out what the re module does, but if you save this script under the name re.py, you'll get a mysterious error when you run your program:

```
$ python re.py
Regular Expression: [0-9]+
String: test123abc
Traceback (most recent call last):
...
File "./re.py", line 9, in <module>
    results = re.search(pattern, s)
AttributeError: 'module' object has no attribute 'search'
```

Can you figure out what's going on here? The answer lies, once again, in the module search path. The name of your script, re.py, is masking the re module in the Python Standard Library, so when your program attempts to import the re module, it actually loads itself instead. You're seeing an AttributeError here because the script successfully loaded itself as a module but that module doesn't have the search() function you were expecting.

Having a script import itself as a module can also cause unexpected problems; we'll look at this shortly.

The solution to this problem is simple: never use the name of a Python Standard Library module for a script. Instead, call your test script something like `re_test.py`.

Adding package directories to sys.path

A common trap to fall into is adding a package directory to `sys.path`. Let's take a look at what happens when you do this.

Create a directory to hold a test program, and create a sub-directory named `package` within this main directory. Then, create an empty package initialization (`__init__.py`) file within the `package` directory. Also, create a module, named `module.py`, within the same directory. Then, add the following to the `module.py` file:

```
print("### Initializing module.py ###")
```

This prints out a message when the module is imported. Next, create a Python source file named `good_imports.py` in your top-most directory, and enter the following Python code into this file:

```
print("Calling import package.module...")
import package.module
print("Calling import package.module as module...")
import package.module as module
print("Calling from package import module...")
from package import module
```

After saving this file, open a terminal or command-line window and use the `cd` command to set the current directory to your outermost directory (the one containing your `good_imports.py` script), and type `python good_imports.py` to run this program. You should see the following output:

```
$ python good_imports.py
Calling import package.module...
### Initializing module.py ###
Calling import package.module as module...
Calling from package import module...
```

As you can see, the first `import` statement loaded the module, which caused the `### Initializing module.py ###` message to be printed out. For the subsequent `import` statements, no initialization took place—instead, the already-imported copy of the module was used. This is the behavior we want as it ensures that we only ever have one copy of each module. This is important for those modules that keep information in global variables as having different copies of a module with different values in their global variables can lead to all sorts of strange and confusing behavior.

Unfortunately, that's exactly what we can end up with if we add a package, or a sub-directory of a package, to `sys.path`. To see this problem in action, create a new top-level script named `bad_imports.py`, and enter the following into this file:

```
import os.path
import sys

cur_dir = os.path.abspath(os.path.dirname(__file__))
package_dir = os.path.join(cur_dir, "package")

sys.path.insert(1, package_dir)

print("Calling import package.module as module...")
import package.module as module
print("Calling import module...")
import module
```

This program sets `package_dir` to the full directory path to the `package` directory and then adds this directory to `sys.path`. It then makes two separate `import` statements, one to import `module` from the package named `package` and the other to import `module` directly. Both `import` statements will work as the module can be accessed in both ways. However, the results are not what you might expect:

```
$ python bad_imports.py
Calling import package.module as module...
### Initializing module.py ###
Calling import module...
### Initializing module.py ###
```

As you can see, the module is imported *twice*, once as `package.module` and again as `module`. You end up with two separate copies of the module, both of which are initialized and appear as two distinct modules to the Python system.

Having two copies of a module can lead to all sorts of subtle bugs and problems. This is why you should never add a Python package, or a sub-directory of a Python package, directly to `sys.path`.

> Of course, it's fine to add a directory *containing* a package to `sys.path`; just don't add the package directory itself.

Executing and importing the same module

Another more subtle example of the double-import problem can occur if you execute a Python source file and then import that same file as if it were a module. To see how this works, create a directory to hold a new example program, and create a new Python source file in this directory named `test.py`. Then, enter the following into this file:

```
import helpers

def do_something(n):
    return n * 2

if __name__ == "__main__":
    helpers.run_test()
```

When this file is run as a script, it calls the `helpers.run_test()` function to start running a test. This file also defines a function, `do_something()`, that performs some useful functionality. Now, create a second Python source file in the same directory named `helpers.py`, and enter the following into this file:

```
import test

def run_test():
    print(test.do_something(10))
```

As you can see, the `helpers.py` module is importing `test.py` as a module and then calling the `do_something()` function as part of running the test. In other words, even though `test.py` is executed as a script, it is also being imported (indirectly) as a module as part of the execution of that script.

Let's see what happens when you run this program:

```
$ python test.py
20
```

So far so good. The program is running and, despite the convoluted module imports, it seems to be working. But let's take a closer look; add the following statement to the top of your `test.py` script:

```
print("Initializing test.py")
```

As in our previous example, we are using a `print()` statement to show when the module is being loaded. This gives the module the opportunity to initialize itself, and we would expect to only see the initialization happen once as there should only ever be one copy of each module in memory.

In this case, however, that's not what happens. Try running the program again:

```
$ python test.py
Initializing test.py
Initializing test.py
20
```

As you can see, the module is being initialized *twice* — once when it's run as a script and again when the module is imported by `helpers.py`.

To avoid this problem, make sure that any scripts you write are only used as scripts. Keep any other code (such as the `do_something()` function from our previous example) out of your scripts so that you'll never need to import them.

Note that this doesn't mean that you can't have chameleon modules that act as both a module and as a script, as described in *Chapter 3, Using Modules and Packages*. Just be careful that the script you execute only uses functions defined within the module itself. If you start importing other modules from the same package, you should probably move all the functionality into a different module, which you then import into your script, rather than having them both together in the same file.

Using modules and packages with the Python interactive interpreter

As well as calling modules and packages from a Python script, it is often useful to call them directly from the Python interactive interpreter. This is a great way of employing the **rapid application development (RAD)** technique for Python programming: you make a change of some sort to a Python module or package and immediately see the results of your change by calling that module or package from the Python interactive interpreter.

There are, however, a few limitations and issues to be aware of. Let's take a closer look at how you can use the interactive interpreter to speed up your development of modules and packages; we'll also see where a different approach might suit you better.

Start by creating a new Python module named `stringutils.py`, and enter the following code into this file:

```python
import re

def extract_numbers(s):
    pattern = r'[+-]?\d+(?:\.\d+)?'
    numbers = []
    for match in re.finditer(pattern, s):
        number = s[match.start:match.end+1]
        numbers.append(number)
    return numbers
```

This module represents our first attempt at writing a function to extract all the numbers from a string. Note that it is not working yet—the `extract_numbers()` function will crash if you try to use it. It's also not particularly efficient (a much easier approach would be to use the `re.findall()` function). But we're using this code deliberately to show how you can apply rapid application development techniques to your Python modules, so bear with us.

This function uses the `re` (regular expression) module to find the parts of the string that match the given expression pattern. The complicated `pattern` string is used to match a number, including an optional + or - at the front, any number of digits, and an optional fractional part at the end.

Using the `re.finditer()` function, we find the parts of the string that match our regular expression pattern. We then extract each matching part of the string and append the results to the `numbers` list, which we then return back to the caller.

So much for what our function is supposed to do. Let's test it out.

Open a terminal or command-line window, and use the `cd` command to switch to the directory holding the `stringutils.py` module. Then, type `python` to start up the Python interactive interpreter. When the Python command prompt appears, try entering the following:

```
>>> import stringutils
>>> print(stringutils.extract_numbers("Tes1t 123.543 -10.6 5"))
Traceback (most recent call last):
  File "<stdin>", line 1, in <module>
  File "./stringutils.py", line 7, in extract_numbers
    number = s[match.start:match.end+1]
TypeError: unsupported operand type(s) for +: 'builtin_function_or_
method' and 'int'
```

As you can see, our module doesn't work yet—we have a bug in it. Looking closer, we can see that the problem is on line 7 of our `stringutils.py` module:

```
number = s[match.start:match.end+1]
```

The error message suggests that you are trying to add a built-in function (in this case, `match.end`) to a number (1), which of course doesn't work. The `match.start` and `match.end` values were supposed to be the indices into the string for the start and end of the number, but a quick look at the documentation for the `re` module shows that `match.start` and `match.end` are functions, not simple numbers, and so we need to call these functions to get the values we want. Doing this is easy; simply edit line 7 of your file to look like the following:

```
number = s[match.start():match.end()+1]
```

Now that we've changed our module, let's take a look at what happens. We'll start by re-executing the `print()` statement to see if that works:

```
>>> print(stringutils.extract_numbers("Tes1t 123.543 -10.6 5"))
```

 Did you know that you can press the up arrow and down arrow keys on your keyboard to move through the history of commands that you've typed previously into the Python interactive interpreter? This saves you from having to retype a command; simply use the arrow keys to select the command you want, and press *Return* to execute it.

You'll immediately see the same error message you saw previously—nothing has changed. This is because you imported the module into the Python interpreter; once a module or package has been imported, it is held in memory and the source file(s) on disk are ignored.

To have your changes take effect, you need to **reload** the module. To do this, type the following into your Python interpreter:

```
import importlib
```

```
importlib.reload(stringutils)
```

 If you are using Python 2.x, you can't use the `importlib` module. Instead, simply type `reload(stringutils)`. If you are using Python version 3.3, use `imp` rather than `importlib`.

Now try re-executing that `print()` statement:

```
>>> stringutils.extract_numbers("Helllo 123.543 -10.6 5 there")
['1o', '123.543 ', '-10.6 ', '5 ']
```

That's much better—our program now runs without crashing. There is, however, one more problem we need to fix: when we extract the characters that make up a number, we're extracting one character too many, so the number 1 is being returned as 1o and so on. To fix this, remove the +1 from line 7 of your source file:

```
number = s[match.start():match.end()]
```

Then, reload the module again and re-execute your `print()` statement. You should see the following:

```
['1', '123.543', '-10.6', '5']
```

Perfect! If you wanted to, you could use the `float()` function to convert these strings into floating-point numbers, but for our purposes this module is now finished.

Let's take a step back and review what we've done. We had a module with mistakes in it, and used the Python interactive interpreter to help identify and fix these problems. We repeatedly tested our program, noticed a mistake, and fixed it, using a RAD approach to quickly find and correct the bugs in our module.

When developing your modules and packages, it's often helpful to test them in the interactive interpreter to find and fix problems as you go along. You just have to remember that every time you make a change to a Python source file, you'll need to call `importlib.reload()` to reload the affected module or package.

Using the Python interactive interpreter in this way also means that you have the complete Python system available for your testing. For example, you could use the `pprint` module in the Python Standard Library to pretty-print a complex dictionary or list so that you can easily view the information being returned by one of your functions.

There are some limitations, however, in the `importlib.reload()` process:

- Imagine that you have two modules, A and B. Module A uses the `from B import...` statement to load functionality from module B. If you then change module B, the changed functionality won't be used by module A unless you reload that module too.

- If your module crashes while initializing itself, it can end up in a strange state. For example, imagine that your module includes the following top-level code, which is supposed to initialize a list of customers:

```
customers = []
customers.append("Mike Wallis")
cusotmers.append("John Smith")
```

  This module will be imported, but because of the misspelled variable name it will raise an exception during initialization. If this happens, you will need to firstly use the `import` command in the Python interactive interpreter to make the module available, and then use `imp.reload()` to load the updated source code.

- Because you have to either type the commands yourself or select a command from the Python command history, it can get tedious to run the same code over and over, especially if your test involves more than a couple of steps. It's also very easy to miss a step when using the interactive interpreter.

For these reasons, it is best to use the interactive interpreter to fix specific problems or to help you rapidly develop a particular small piece of code. Custom written scripts work better when the tests get complicated or if you have to work with multiple modules.

Dealing with global variables

We have already seen how to use global variables to share information between different functions within a module. We've seen how to define globals as top-level variables within a module, causing them to be initialized the first time the module is imported, and we have also seen how to use the `global` statement within a function to allow that function to access and change the value of a global variable.

In this section, we will build on this knowledge to learn how to share global variables *between* modules. When creating a package, you often need to define variables that can be accessed or changed by any module within that package. Sometimes, you also need to make a variable available to Python code outside your package. Let's take a look at how this can be done.

Create a new directory named `globtest`, and create an empty package initialization file inside this directory to make it a Python package. Then, create a file inside this directory named `globals.py`, and enter the following into this file:

```
language = None
currency = None
```

In this module, we have defined two global variables that we want to use in our package, and given each variable a default value of None. Let's now use these globals in another module.

Create another file in the globtest directory named test.py, and enter the following into this file:

```
from . import globals

def test():
    globals.language = "EN"
    globals.currency = "USD"
    print(globals.language, globals.currency)
```

To test your program, open a terminal or command-line window, use the cd command to move to the directory that contains your globtest package, and type python to start up the Python interactive interpreter. Then, try entering the following:

```
>>> from globtest import test
>>> test.test()
EN USD
```

As you can see, we have successfully set the value of the language and currency globals, which are stored in our globals module, and then retrieved these values again to print them out. Because we are storing these globals in a separate module, you can retrieve or change these globals anywhere within the current package or even in other code that imports your package. Using a separate module to hold your package's global variables is an excellent way of managing globals within a package.

There is, however, one thing to be aware of: for a global variable to be shared between modules, you must import the *module* that contains that global variable, not the variable itself. For example, the following won't work:

```
from .test import language
```

What this statement does is import a copy of the language variable into your current module's global namespace, not the original global. This means that the global variable won't be shared with other modules. For a variable to be shared between modules, you need to import the globals module, not the variables within it.

Package configuration

As you develop more sophisticated modules and packages, you will often find that your code needs to be *configured* in some way before it can be used. For example, imagine that you're writing a package that uses a database. To do this, your package needs to know which database engine to use, the name of the database, and the username and password to use to access that database.

You could hardwire this information into your program's source code, but doing this is a very bad idea, for two reasons:

- Different computers and different operating systems will use different database setups. Since the information used to access the database will vary from one computer to another, anyone wanting to use your package would have to edit the source code directly to enter the correct database details before the package can be run.

- The username and password used to access a database is highly sensitive information. If you share your package with other people, or even just store a copy of your package's source code on a public repository such as GitHub, then other people can discover your database access credentials. This is a huge security risk.

These database access credentials are an example of *package configuration* — information that your package needs before it can run but which you don't want to build into your package's source code.

If you are building an application rather than a standalone module or package, your configuration task is much simpler. There are modules in the Python Standard Library that can help with configuration, for example, `configparser`, `shlex`, and `json`. Using these modules, you can store configuration settings in a file on disk, which the end user can edit. When your program starts, you load those settings into memory and access them as needed. Because the configuration settings are stored externally to your application, users won't have to edit your source code to configure the program, and you won't be exposing sensitive information if your source code is published or shared.

When writing modules and packages, however, the file-based approach to configuration is much less convenient. There's no obvious place to store a package's configuration file, and requiring configuration files at a particular location is going to make your module or package harder to reuse as part of a different program.

Instead, configuration for a module or package is usually done by supplying parameters to your module or package's initialization function. We saw an example of this in the previous chapter, where the quantities package required you to supply a locale value when initializing the package:

```
quantities.init("us")
```

This passes the job of configuration back to the surrounding application; the application can make use of a configuration file, or any other configuration scheme it likes, and it is the application that supplies the package's configuration settings when the package is initialized:

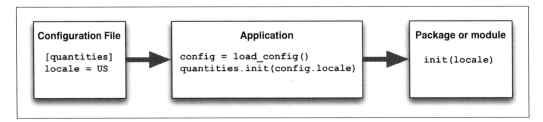

This makes things easier for the package developer as all the package needs to do is remember the settings it has been given.

While the quantities package only used a single configuration setting (the name of the locale), it is common for packages to use many settings. A very convenient way of supplying the configuration settings for a package is to use a Python dictionary. For example:

```
mypackage.init({'log_errors'  : True,
                'db_password' : "test123",
                ...})
```

Using a dictionary in this way makes it easy to support *default values* for your package's configuration settings. The following Python snippet shows how a package's init() function can accept configuration settings, supply default values, and store the settings in a global variable so that it can be accessed when needed:

```
def init(settings):
    global config

    config = {}
    config['log_errors']  = settings.get("log_errors",  False)
    config['db_password'] = settings.get("db_password", "")
    ...
```

Using `dict.get()` in this way, you retrieve the setting if one has been supplied, while providing a default value to use if the setting isn't specified. This is an ideal way of handling configuration within a Python module or package, making it simple for users of your module or package to configure it as required, while still leaving the details of how and where the configuration settings are stored up to the application.

Package data

A package might contain more than just Python source files. Sometimes, you might need to include other types of files as well. For example, a package may include one or more image files, a large text file containing a list of all the ZIP codes in the USA, or any other type of data you may need. If you can store something in a file, you can include this file as part of your Python package.

Normally, you would place your package data in a separate sub-directory within the package directory. To access these files, your package needs to know where to find this sub-directory. While you could hardwire the location of this directory into your package, this won't work if your package is to be reused or moved. It's also not necessary as you can easily find the directory in which a module resides by using the following code:

```
cur_dir = os.path.abspath(os.path.dirname(__file__))
```

This gives you the complete path to the directory containing the current module. Using the `os.path.join()` function, you can then get access to the sub-directory that holds your data files and open them in the usual way:

```
phone_numbers = []
cur_dir = os.path.abspath(os.path.dirname(__file__))
file = open(os.path.join(cur_dir, "data", "phone_numbers.txt"))
for line in file:
    phone_numbers.append(line.strip())
file.close()
```

The great thing about including data files inside your package is that the data files are effectively part of your package's source code. When you share your package or upload it to a source code repository such as GitHub, the data files are automatically included along with the rest of your package. This makes it much easier to keep track of the data files used by your package.

Summary

In this chapter, we looked at a number of the more advanced aspects of working with modules and packages in Python. We saw how a `try..except` statement can be used to implement optional imports, and how an `import` statement can be placed inside a function so that the module only gets imported when that function is executed. We then learned about the module search path and how you can modify `sys.path` to change the way the Python interpreter looks for modules and packages.

We then looked at some of the gotchas related to the use of modules and packages. We learned about name masking, where you define a module or package with the same name as a module or package in the Python Standard Library, which can lead to unexpected failures. We looked at how giving a Python script the same name as a Standard Library module can also cause name masking problems, and how adding a package directory or sub-directory to `sys.path` can cause a module to be loaded twice, leading to subtle problems with global variables within that module. We saw how executing a module and then importing it also leads to that module being loaded twice, which can again lead to problems.

We next looked at how you can use the Python interactive interpreter as a type of rapid application development (RAD) tool to quickly find and fix problems within your modules and packages, and how the `importib.reload()` command allows you to reload a module after you have changed the underlying source code

We finished our survey of advanced module techniques by learning how to define global variables that are used throughout a package, how to handle package configuration, and how to store and access data files within a package.

In the next chapter, we will look at some of the ways in which you can test, deploy, and share your Python modules and packages.

8

Testing and Deploying Modules

In this chapter, we will delve further into the concept of sharing modules. Before you can share a module or package, you need to test it to ensure that it is working properly. You also need to prepare your code and know how to deploy it. To learn these things, we will cover the following topics:

- See how unit tests can be used to ensure that your module or package is working properly
- Learn how to prepare a module or package for publication
- Find out how GitHub can be used to share your code with others
- Examine the steps involved in submitting your code to the Python Package Index
- Discover how to use pip to install and use packages written by other people

Testing modules and packages

Testing is a normal part of programming: you test your code to verify that it works and identify any bugs or other problems, which you can then fix. Then, you test some more, until you are happy that your code is working correctly.

All too often, however, programmers just do **ad hoc testing**: they fire up the Python interactive interpreter, import their module or package, and make various calls to see what happens. In the previous chapter, we looked at a form of ad hoc testing using the `importlib.reload()` function to support RAD development of your code.

Ad hoc testing is useful, but it isn't the only form of testing. If you are sharing your modules and packages with others, you will want your code to be bug-free, and ad-hoc testing can't guarantee this. A much better and more systematic approach is to create a series of **unit tests** for your module or package. Unit tests are snippets of Python code which test various aspects of your code. Because the testing is done by a Python program, you can simply run the program whenever you want to test your code, and you can be sure that everything is being tested each time you run the test. Unit tests are a great way of making sure bugs don't creep into your code as you make changes, and you can run them whenever you want to share your code to make sure it's working as you expect.

> Unit tests aren't the only sort of programmatic testing you can do. **Integration tests** combine various modules and systems to make sure they work together correctly, and **GUI tests** are used to ensure that a program's user interface is working as it should. Unit tests are, however, the most useful for testing modules and packages, and this is the type of testing we will focus on in this chapter.

The following is a very simple example of a unit test:

```
import math
assert math.floor(2.6197) == 2
```

The `assert` statement checks the expression that follows it. If this expression does not evaluate to `True`, then an `AssertionError` will be raised. This makes it easy for you to check that a given function is returning the results you expect; in this example, we are checking that the `math.floor()` function is correctly returning the largest integer less than or equal to the given floating-point number.

Because a module or package is ultimately just a collection of Python functions (or methods, which are just functions grouped into classes), it is quite possible to write a series of `assert` statements that call your functions and check that the returned values are what you would expect.

Of course, this is a simplification: often the results of calling one function will affect the output of another function, and your functions can sometimes perform quite complex actions such as communicating with a remote API or storing data into a file on disk. In many cases, though, you can still use a series of `assert` statements to verify that your modules and packages are working the way you would expect.

Testing with the unittest Standard Library module

While you could put your `assert` statements into a Python script and run them, a better approach is to use the `unittest` module from the Python Standard Library. This module allows you to group your unit tests into **test cases**, run additional code before and after the tests are run, and access a whole raft of different types of `assert` statements to make your testing easier.

Let's see how we can use the `unittest` module to implement a series of unit tests for the `quantities` package we implemented in *Chapter 6, Creating Reusable Modules*. Place a copy of this package into a convenient directory and create a new Python source file named `test_quantities.py` in the same directory. Then, add the following code to this file:

```python
import unittest
import quantities

class TestQuantities(unittest.TestCase):
    def setUp(self):
        quantities.init("us")

    def test_new(self):
        q = quantities.new(12, "km")
        self.assertEqual(quantities.value(q), 12)
        self.assertEqual(quantities.units(q), "kilometer")

    def test_convert(self):
        q1 = quantities.new(12, "km")
        q2 = quantities.convert(q1, "m")
        self.assertEqual(quantities.value(q2), 12000)
        self.assertEqual(quantities.units(q2), "meter")

if __name__ == "__main__":
    unittest.main()
```

 Remember that you don't need to type this program in by hand. All of these source files, including a complete copy of the `quantities` package, are available as part of the sample code which can be downloaded for this chapter.

Let's take a closer look at what this code does. First off, the `TestQuantities` class is used to hold a number of related unit tests. You would normally define a separate `unittest.TestCase` subclass for each of the major groups of unit tests that you need to perform. Within our `TestQuantities` class, we define a `setUp()` method which contains code that needs to be executed before our tests are run. If we wanted to, we could also define a `tearDown()` method that would be executed after the tests have been completed.

We then define two unit tests, which we have called `test_new()` and `test_convert()`. These test the `quantities.new()` and `quantities.convert()` functions, respectively. You would typically have a separate unit test for each piece of functionality that you need to test. You can call your unit tests anything you like, so long as the method name starts with `test`.

Within our `test_new()` unit test, we create a new quantity and then call the `self.assertEqual()` method to ensure that the expected quantity was created. As you can see, we're not just limited to using the built-in `assert` statement; there are dozens of different `assertXXX()` methods that you can call to test your code in various ways. All of these will raise an `AssertionError` if the assertion fails.

The last part of our testing script calls `unittest.main()` when the script is executed. This function looks for any `unittest.TestCase` sub-classes that you have defined and runs each test case in turn. For each test case, the `setUp()` method is called if it exists, followed by the various `testXXX()` methods that you have defined, and finally, the `teardown()` method is called if it exists.

Let's try running our unit test. Open up a terminal or command-line window, use the `cd` command to set the current directory to the directory holding your `test_quantities.py` script, and try typing the following:

python test_quantities.py

All going well, you should see the following output:

```
..
----------------------------------------------------------------------
Ran 2 tests in 0.000s


OK
```

By default, the `unittest` module doesn't show you much about the tests that have been run, other than that it ran your unit tests without any problems. If you want more detail, you can increase the **verbosity** of your tests, for example by adding a parameter to the `unittest.main()` statement in your test script:

```
unittest.main(verbosity=2)
```

Alternatively, you can use the `-v` command-line option to achieve the same result:

```
python test_quantities.py -v
```

Designing your unit tests

The aim of unit testing is to check that your code is working. A good rule of thumb is to have a separate test case for each publicly accessible module within your package and a separate unit test for each feature provided by that module. The unit test code should aim to test at least the usual operation of the feature to make sure it works. If you wish, you can also choose to write additional testing code within your unit tests, or even additional unit tests, to check for particular **edge cases** in your code.

To use a concrete example, in the `test_convert()` method we wrote in the previous section, you might want to add code to check that a suitable exception is raised if the user tries to convert a distance into a weight. For example:

```
q = quantities.new(12, "km")
with self.assertRaises(ValueError):
    quantities.convert(q, "kg")
```

The question is: how many edge cases should you test for? There are potentially hundreds of different ways in which someone can use your module incorrectly. Should you write unit tests for each of these?

In general, no. It isn't worth your while trying to test every possible edge case. Certainly, you may wish to test a few of the main possibilities, just to make sure your module is able to handle the most obvious errors, but beyond this, writing additional tests probably isn't worth the effort.

Code coverage

Coverage is a measure of how much of your code is being tested by your unit tests. To understand how this works, consider the following Python function:

```
[1] def calc_score(x, y):
[2]     if x == 1:
[3]         score = y * 10
[4]     elif x == 2:
```

```
[5]              score = 25 + y
[6]        else:
[7]              score = y
[8]
[9]        return score
```

 We have added line numbers to the start of each line to help us calculate the code coverage.

Now, imagine that we create the following unit test code for our `calc_score()` function:

```
assert calc_score(1, 5) == 50
assert calc_score(2, 10) == 35
```

How much of the `calc_score()` function has our unit test covered? Our first `assert` statement is calling `calc_score()` with x as 1 and y as 5. If you follow the line numbers, you'll see that calling this function with this set of parameters will cause lines 1, 2, 3, and 9 to be executed. Similarly, the second `assert` statement calls `calc_score()` with x as 2 and y as 10, causing lines 1, 4, 5, and 9 to be executed.

In total, these two assert statements caused lines 1, 2, 3, 4, 5, and 9 to be executed. Ignoring the blank line, our test did not include lines 6 and 7. Thus, our unit test has covered six of the eight lines in our function, giving us a code coverage value of 6/8 = 75%.

 We are looking at **statement coverage** here. There are other, more complicated, ways of measuring code coverage which we won't get into here.

Obviously, you won't calculate code coverage by hand. There are some excellent tools that will calculate code coverage for your Python testing code. Take a look, for example, at the `coverage` package (`https://pypi.python.org/pypi/coverage`).

The basic concept of code coverage is that you want your tests to cover *all* your code. Whether or not you use a tool such as `coverage` to measure code coverage, it's a good idea to write your unit tests to include as close to 100% of your code as possible.

Test-driven development

While we are looking at the idea of testing Python code, it is worth mentioning the concept of **test-driven development**. Using test-driven development, you first choose what you want your module or package to do, and then you write unit tests to ensure that the module or package works the way you want it to—*before you write it*. In this way, the unit tests act as a kind of specification for the module or package; they tell you what your code should do, and your task is then to write the code so that it passes all the tests.

Test-driven development can be a useful way of implementing your modules and packages. Whether or not you use it, of course, is up to you—but if you have the discipline to write the unit tests first, test-driven development can be a great way of making sure you've implemented your code correctly, and your modules continue to do what you expect them to as your code grows and changes over time.

Mocking

If your module or package calls an external API or performs some other complex, expensive, or time-consuming operation, you may want to investigate the `unittest.mock` package in the Python Standard Library. **Mocking** is the process of replacing some functionality in your program with a dummy function that immediately returns suitable data for testing.

Mocking is a complicated process, and it can take some doing to get it right, but the technique is absolutely worthwhile if you want to run unit tests over code that would otherwise be too slow, cost money each time you ran it, or depends on external systems to operate.

Writing unit tests for your modules and packages

Now that we have been introduced to the concept of unit testing, taken a look at how the `unittest` standard library module works, and looked at some of the more complicated but important aspects of writing unit tests, let's now see how unit tests can be used to assist with the development and testing of your modules and packages.

First off, you should aim to write unit tests for at least the main functions defined by your module or package. Start by testing the most important functions, and add tests for the more obvious error conditions to make sure errors are being handled correctly. You can always add extra tests for the more obscure parts of your code later.

If you are writing unit tests for a single module, you should place your test code in a separate Python script, named, for example, `tests.py`, and place this in the same directory as your module. The following image shows a good way of organizing your code when writing a single module:

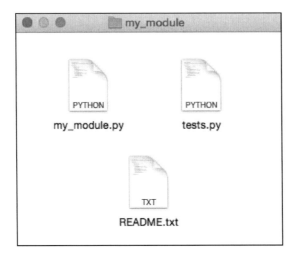

If you have multiple modules in the same directory, you can either combine the unit tests for all the modules into the `tests.py` script, or else rename it to something like `test_my_module.py` to make it clear which module is being tested.

For a package, make sure you place the `tests.py` script in the directory that contains the package, not inside the package itself:

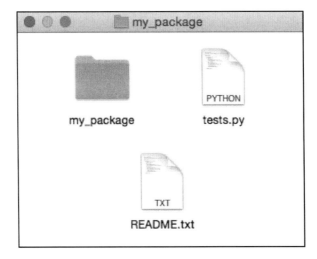

If you place the `test.py` script inside the package directory, you are likely to encounter problems when your unit tests attempt to import the package.

Your `tests.py` script should define a `unittest.TestCase` object for each publicly accessible module in your package, and each of these objects should have a `testXXX()` method for each function or major piece of functionality defined within the module.

Doing this allows you to test your module or package simply by executing the following command:

```
python test.py
```

You should run your unit tests whenever you want to check that your module is working, and in particular before uploading or sharing your module or package with other people.

Preparing a module or package for publication

In *Chapter 6*, *Creating Reusable Modules*, we looked at a number of things that make a module or package suitable for reuse:

- It must function as a standalone unit
- A package should ideally use relative imports
- Any external dependencies in your module or package must be clearly noted

We also identified three things that help to create an excellent reusable module or package:

- It should solve a general problem
- Your code should follow standard coding conventions
- Your module or package should be clearly documented

The first step in preparing your module or package for publication is to ensure that you've followed at least the first three of these, and, ideally, all six of these guidelines.

The second step is to make sure that you've written at least a few unit tests and your module or package passes all of these. Finally, you will need to decide *how* you want to publish your code.

If you want to share your code with friends or work colleagues or write a blog post along with a link to your code, then the easiest way to do so is to upload it to a source code repository such as GitHub. We will take a look at how this is done in the next section. Unless you make it private, your code can be accessed by anyone who has the correct link. People can view your source code (including the documentation) online, download your module or package for use in their own programs, and "fork" your code, creating their own private copy which they can then modify.

If you want to share your code with a wider audience, the best approach is to submit it to the **Python Package Index (PyPI)**. This will mean that others can find your module or package by searching through the PyPI index and anyone can install it using **pip**, the Python Package Manager. Later sections of this chapter will describe how to submit your module or package to PyPI and how pip can be used to download and work with modules and packages.

Uploading your work to GitHub

GitHub (`https://github.com/`) is a popular web-based system for storing and managing source code. While there are several alternatives, GitHub is particularly popular with people writing and sharing open source Python code, and this is the source code management system that we will use in this book.

Before delving into the specifics of GitHub, let's start by looking at how source code management systems work in general and why you might want to use one.

Imagine that you are writing a complex module and have opened your module in a text editor to make a few changes. While making these changes, you accidentally select 100 lines of code and press the *Delete* key. Before you realize what you've done, you save and close the file. Too late: those 100 lines of text are gone.

Of course, you might (and hopefully will) have a backup system in place which keeps regular backups of your source files. But if you had made changes to some of the missing code in the past few minutes, you are likely to have lost those changes.

Now consider a situation where you've shared a module or package with a colleague, and they decide to make a few changes. Perhaps there's a bug that needed fixing or a new feature they wanted to add. They change your code and send it back to you with a note describing what they've done. Unfortunately, unless you compare each line in the original and modified versions of your source files, you can't be sure exactly what your colleague has done to your files.

A source code management system solves these types of problems. Instead of just having a copy of your module or package sitting in a directory on your hard disk, you create a **repository** within a source code management system such as GitHub, and **commit** your source code to this repository. Then, as you make changes to your files, fixing bugs and adding features, you commit each change that you make back to the repository. The source code repository keeps track of every change you have made, allowing you to see exactly what has been changed over time and, where necessary, undoing changes that were made previously.

You aren't limited to having just one person work on a module or package. People can **fork** your source code repository, creating their own private copy of it, and then use this private copy to fix bugs and add new features. Once they've done this, they can send you a **pull request** which includes the changes they have made. You can then decide whether or not to merge those changes into your project.

Don't worry too much about these details, though—source code management is a complex topic, and there are lots of sophisticated tricks you can perform using tools such as GitHub to manage your source code. The important thing to remember is that you create a repository to hold the master copy of the source code for your module or package, commit your code into this repository, and then continue to commit each time you fix a bug or add a new feature. The following illustration summarizes this process:

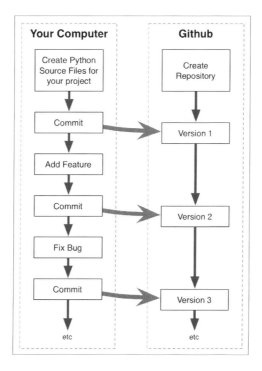

The trick with a source management system is to commit regularly—every time you add a new feature or fix a bug, you should immediately commit your changes. This way, the difference between one version and the next in the repository is only the code which adds that one feature or fixes that one problem. If you make a number of changes to your source code before committing, the repository will be a lot less useful.

Now that we've seen how source code management systems work, let's implement a real example to see how to use GitHub for managing your source code. First off, go to the main GitHub site (`https://github.com/`). If you don't have an account with GitHub, you will need to sign up, choosing a unique username, as well as supplying a contact e-mail address and password. If you have used GitHub before, you can sign in with the username and password you have already set up.

Note that it's free to sign up and use GitHub; the only limitation is that every repository you create will be public, so anyone who wishes to can see your source code. You can set up private repositories if you want, but these do incur a monthly charge. However, since we are using GitHub to share our code with others, having a private repository doesn't make any sense. You'd only need a private (paid) repository if you wanted to share your code with a select group of people while preventing anyone else from accessing it. If you're in the position of having to do this, though, paying for a private repository is the least of your concerns.

Once you have signed in to GitHub, your next task is to install the command-line tools for **Git**. Git is the underlying source code management toolkit used by GitHub; you'll use the `git` command to work with your GitHub repository from the command line.

To install the required software, go to `https://git-scm.com/downloads` and download an installer for your particular operating system. Once this has finished downloading, run the installer and follow the instructions as it installs the `git` command-line tools. When this is finished, open a terminal or command-line window, and try typing the following command:

```
git --version
```

All going well, you should see the version number of the `git` command-line tools you have installed.

With these prerequisites out of the way, let's use GitHub to create an example repository. Go back to the `https://github.com/` web page and click on the **+ New Repository** button highlighted in green. You will be asked to enter the details of the repository you want to create:

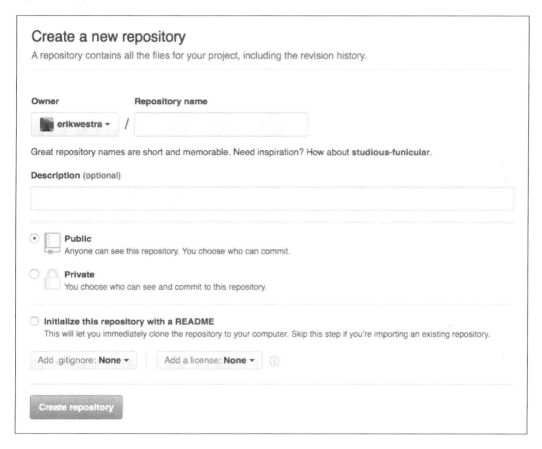

To set up your repository, enter `test-package` for the repository's name, and choose **Python** from the **Add .gitignore** drop-down menu. A `.gitignore` file is used to exclude certain files from the repository; using a `.gitignore` file for Python means that the temporary files Python creates won't be included in the repository.

Finally, click on the **Create repository** button to create the new repository.

> Make sure you don't select the **Initialize this repository with a README** option. You don't want a README file created at this stage; the reason for this will become clear shortly.

Now that the repository has been created on GitHub, our next task is to **clone** a copy of that repository onto your computer's hard disk. To do this, create a new directory named `test-package` to hold your local copy of the repository, open up a terminal or command-line window, and use the `cd` command to move to your new `test-package` directory. Then, type the following command:

```
git clone https://<username>@github.com/<username>/test-package.git .
```

Make sure you replace both instances of `<username>` in the preceding command with your GitHub username. You will be prompted to enter your GitHub password to authenticate yourself, and a copy of the repository will be saved into your new directory.

Because the repository is currently empty, you won't see anything in your directory. However, there are some hidden files that `git` uses to keep track of your local copy of the repository. To see these hidden files, you can use the `ls` command from a terminal window:

```
$ ls -al
drwxr-xr-x@  7 erik  staff   238 19 Feb 21:28 .
drwxr-xr-x@  7 erik  staff   238 19 Feb 14:35 ..
drwxr-xr-x@ 14 erik  staff   476 19 Feb 21:28 .git
-rw-r--r--@  1 erik  staff   844 19 Feb 15:09 .gitignore
```

The `.git` directory holds information about your new GitHub repository, while the `.gitignore` file contains the instructions you asked GitHub to set up for you to ignore the Python temporary files.

Now that we have an (initially empty) repository, let's create some files in it. The first thing we need to do is choose a unique name for our package. Because our package is going to be submitted to the Python Package Index, the name must be truly unique. To achieve this, we'll use your GitHub username as the basis for our package name, like this:

```
<username>-test-package
```

For example, since my GitHub username is "erikwestra", the name I would use for this package would be `erikwestra-test-package`. Make sure you select a name based on your GitHub username, to make sure that the package name is truly unique.

Now that we have a name for our package, let's create a README file describing this package. Create a new text file named `README.rst` in your `test-package` directory, and place the following into this file:

```
<username>-test-package
-----------------------


This is a simple test package. To use it, type::

    from <username>_test_package import test
    test.run()
```

Make sure you replace each occurrence of `<username>` with your GitHub username. This text file is in **reStructuredText format**. reStructuredText is a formatting language used by PyPI to display formatted text.

 While GitHub can support reStructuredText, by default it uses a different text format called **Markdown**. Markdown and reStructuredText are two competing formats, and unfortunately, PyPI requires reStructuredText, while GitHub by default uses Markdown. This is why we told GitHub not to create a README file when we set up the repository; if we had done this, it would have been in the wrong format.

When the user views your repository on GitHub, they will see the contents of this file neatly formatted according to the reStructuredText rules:

erikwestra-test-package

This is a simple test package. To use it, type:

```
from erikwestra_test_package import test
test.run()
```

If you want to learn more about reStructuredText, you can read all about it at `http://docutils.sourceforge.net/rst.html`.

Now that we have set up the README file for our package, let's create the package itself. Create another directory inside test-package named <username>_test_ package, replacing <username> with your GitHub username, and place an empty package initialization file (__init__.py) inside this directory. Then, create another file inside the <username>_test_package directory named test.py, and enter the following into this file:

```
import string
import random

def random_name():
    chars = []
    for i in range(random.randrange(3, 10)):
        chars.append(random.choice(string.ascii_letters))
    return "".join(chars)


def run():
    for i in range(10):
        print(random_name())
```

This is just an example, of course. Calling the test.run() function will cause ten random names to be displayed. More interesting is the fact that we have now defined the initial contents for our test package. However, all we've done is created some files on our local computer; this doesn't affect GitHub at all, and if you reload your repository page in GitHub, none of your new files will show up.

To have our changes take effect, we need to **commit** our changes to the repository. We'll start by taking a look at how our local copy differs from the one in the repository. To do this, go back to your terminal window, cd into the test-package directory, and type the following command:

`git status`

You should see the following output:

```
# On branch master
# Untracked files:
#   (use "git add <file>..." to include in what will be committed)
#
#   README.rst
#   <username>_test_package/
nothing added to commit but untracked files present (use "git add" to
track)
```

The description can be a bit confusing, but it's not too tricky. Basically, GitHub is telling you that there's a new file, README.rst, and a new directory, named <username>_test_package, which it doesn't know about (or, in GitHub parlance, is "untracked"). Let's add these new entries to our repository:

```
git add README.rst
```

```
git add <username>_test_package
```

Make sure you replace <username> with your GitHub username. If you now type git status, you'll see that the files we created have been added to our local copy of the repository:

```
# On branch master
# Changes to be committed:
#   (use "git reset HEAD <file>..." to unstage)
#
#   new file:   README.rst
#   new file:   <username>_test_package/__init__.py
#   new file:   <username>_test_package/test.py
```

Whenever you add a new directory or file to your project, you will need to use the git add command to add it to the repository. At any time, you can see if you've missed any files by typing the git status command and looking for "untracked" files.

Now that we've included our new files, let's commit our changes to the repository. Type the following command:

```
git commit -a -m 'Initial commit.'
```

This commits a new change to your local copy of the repository. The -a option tells GitHub to automatically include any changed files, and the -m option lets you enter a brief message, describing the changes you have made. In this case, our commit message is set to the value "Initial commit.".

Now that we've committed our change, we need to upload from our local computer to the GitHub repository. To do this, type the following command:

```
git push
```

You will be prompted to enter your GitHub password to authenticate yourself, and the changes you have committed will be stored into your repository on GitHub.

GitHub separates the commit command from the push command because you might need to make several commits as you make changes to your program, without necessarily being online at the time. For example, if you are on a long plane trip, you could work on your code locally, committing each change as you went along and then pushing all your changes at once when you land and have Internet access again.

Now that your changes have been pushed to the server, you can reload the page on GitHub, and your newly created package will appear in the repository:

You will also see the contents of your README.rst file displayed below the list of files, describing your new package and how to use it.

Whenever you make changes to your package, make sure you run through the following steps to save your changes into the repository:

1. Use the git status command to see what's changed. If you've added any files that need to be included in the repository, use git add to add them.
2. Use the git commit -a -m '<commit message>' command to commit your changes to your local copy of the GitHub repository. Make sure you enter a suitable commit message to describe the change you have made.
3. When you are ready to do so, use the git push command to send your committed changes to GitHub.

There's a lot more to using GitHub, of course, and a great many commands and options that you will no doubt want to explore once you get into it—but this is enough to get you started.

Once you've set up a GitHub repository for your Python module or package, it will be easy to share your code with someone else. All you need to do is share a link to your GitHub repository, and the other person can download the files they want.

To make this process even easier and make your packages searchable so that they can be found by a wider audience, you should consider submitting your package to the Python Package Index. We'll look at the steps involved in doing this next.

Submitting to the Python Package Index

To submit your Python package to the Python Package Index, you first have to sign up for a free account at `https://pypi.python.org/pypi`. Click on the **Register** link in the box in the upper-right hand corner of the page:

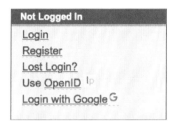

You will need to choose a username and password, as well as supply an e-mail address. Remember the username and password you enter as you'll need it shortly. When you submit the form, you'll be sent an e-mail with a link which you need to click on to complete your registration.

There are two files you will need to add to your project before you can submit it to PyPI, a `setup.py` script, which is used to bundle and upload your package, and a `LICENSE.txt` file, which describes the license under which your package can be used. Let's add these two files now.

Create a file inside your `test-package` directory named `setup.py`, and enter the following into this file:

```
from distutils.core import setup

setup(name="<username>-test-package",
      packages=["<username>_test_package"],
      version="1.0",
      description="Test Package",
      author="<your name>",
      author_email="<your email address>",
      url="https://github.com/<username>/test-package",
      download_url="https://github.com/<username>/test-package/
tarball/1.0",
      keywords=["test", "python"],
      classifiers=[])
```

Make sure you replace each occurrence of `<username>` with your GitHub username, and also replace `<your name>` and `<your email address>` with the relevant values. Because this is just a test, we are using the name `<username>-test-package` for this package; for a real project, we would use a much more meaningful (but still unique) name for our package.

> Notice that this version of the `setup.py` script is using the **Distutils** package. Distutils is part of the Python Standard Library and is a straightforward way of creating and distributing your code. There is an alternative library called **Setuptools**, which many people prefer as it is a more modern library with more features and is often seen as the successor to Distutils. However, Setuptools is not currently part of the Python Standard Library. Since it is easier to use and has all the features we need, we are using Distutils here to keep this process as simple as possible. If you are familiar with using it, feel free to use Setuptools instead of Distutils as the two are identical for what we are doing here.

Finally, we need to create a new text file named `LICENSE.txt`. This file will hold the software license under which you are releasing your package. It is important to include a license so that people know exactly what they can and can't do with your code; you can't submit a package without supplying a license.

While you can put anything you like into the `LICENSE.txt` file, you should generally use one of the existing software licenses. For example, you might like to use the MIT license available at `https://opensource.org/licenses/MIT`—this license makes your code available for others to use for any purpose, while ensuring that you can't be held liable for any problems that may occur from its use.

With these two files in place, you can finally submit your new package to the Python Package Index. To do this, type the following command into your terminal or command-line window:

```
python setup.py register
```

This command will attempt to register your new package with the Python Package Index. You'll be asked to enter your PyPI username and password, and given the opportunity to store these so you don't have to re-enter them each time. Once the package has been successfully registered, you can upload the package contents by typing the following command:

```
python setup.py sdist upload
```

You will see a couple of warnings, which you can safely ignore, before your package is uploaded to PyPI. If you then go to the PyPI web site, you will see your new package listed:

As you can see, the **Home Page** link points to your project's page on GitHub, and there is a direct download link for version 1.0 of your package. Unfortunately, however, this download link doesn't work yet because you haven't told GitHub what version 1.0 of your package looks like. To do this, you have to create a **tag** in GitHub which corresponds to version 1.0 of your system; GitHub will then create a downloadable version of your package that matches that tag.

Before you create your 1.0 release, you should commit the changes you have made to the repository. This is good practice anyway, so let's see how this is done: start by typing `git status` to see which files have been added or changed, then use `git add` to add each of the untracked files in turn. Once this has been done, type `git commit -a -m 'Preparing for PyPI submission'` to commit your changes to the repository. Finally, type `git push` to send your committed changes to GitHub.

Once all this has been done, you can create the tag that corresponds to version 1.0 of your package by typing the following command:

```
git tag 1.0 -m 'Version 1.0 of the <username>_test_package.'
```

Make sure you replace <username> with your GitHub username so that the package name is correct. Finally, use the following variant of the git push command to copy the newly-created tag to the GitHub server:

```
git push --tags
```

Once again, you will be asked to enter your GitHub password. When this command finishes, you will have a version 1.0 release of your package available for download at `https://github.com/<username>/test-package/tarball/1.0`, where <username> is your GitHub username. If you now go to PyPI and look for your test package, you will be able to click on the **Download URL** link to download a copy of your 1.0 package.

If your new package appears in the Python Package Index, and you can successfully download the 1.0 version of your package by following the **Download** link, then you deserve a pat on the back. Congratulations! This is a complex process, but one that will give you the largest audience possible for your reusable modules and packages.

Using pip to download and install modules and packages

In chapters 4 and 5 of this book, we used **pip**, the Python Package Manager, to install various libraries that we wanted to work with. As we learned in *Chapter 7, Advanced Module Techniques*, pip normally installs a package into Python's `site-packages` directory. Since this directory is listed in the module search path, your newly installed module or package can then be imported and used in your code.

Let's now use pip to install the test package we created in the previous section. Since we know that our package has been given the name <username>_test_package, where <username> is your GitHub username, you can install this package directly into your `site-packages` directory by typing the following command into a terminal or command-line window:

```
pip install <username>_test_package
```

Make sure you replace <username> with your GitHub username. Note that if you do not have permission to write to your Python installation's `site-packages` directory, you may need to add `sudo` to the start of this command:

```
sudo pip install <username>_test_package
```

If you do this, you will be prompted to enter your administrator password before the `pip` command is run.

All going well, you should see various commands being run as your newly created package is downloaded and installed. Assuming this works successfully, you can then start your Python interpreter and access your new package just as if it were part of the Python Standard Library. For example:

```
>>> from <username>_test_package import test
>>> test.run()
IFIbH
AAchwnW
qVtRUuSyb
UPF
zXkY
TMJEAZm
wRJCqgomV
oMzmv
LaDeVg
RDfMqScM
```

Of course, it's not just you who can do this. Other Python developers can also access your new package in exactly the same way. This makes it extremely easy for developers to download and use your package.

With a few exceptions, you can use pip to install any package you want from the Python Package Index. By default, pip will install the latest available version of a package; to specify a particular version, you can supply a version number when you install the package, like this:

```
pip install <username>_test_package == 1.0
```

This will install version 1.0 of your test package. If you have already installed a package and a newer version becomes available, you can upgrade your package to the newer version using the `--upgrade` command-line option:

```
pip install --upgrade <username>_test_package
```

You can also obtain a list of the packages you have installed using the `list` command:

```
pip list
```

There is one more feature of pip that you should be aware of. Instead of installing each package individually, you can create a **requirements file** that lists all the packages you want, and have them installed all at once. A typical requirements file would look something like the following:

```
Django==1.8.2
Pillow==3.0.0
reportlab==3.2.0
```

The requirements file lists the various packages you want to have installed and their associated version number.

By convention, a requirements file is named `requirements.txt`, and is placed in your project's top-level directory. Requirements files are extremely useful because they make it easy to recreate a Python development environment, including all the packages that your program depends upon, with just a single command. This is done in the following way:

```
pip install -r requirements.txt
```

Since the requirements file is stored alongside the program's source code, you would normally include the `requirements.txt` file in your source code repository. This means you can clone your repository to a new computer and, with a single command, reinstall all the modules and packages your program depends upon.

While you can create a requirements file by hand, you would normally use pip to create this file for you. After installing the required modules and packages, you can use the following command to create the `requirements.txt` file:

```
pip freeze > requirements.txt
```

The wonderful thing about this command is that you can re-run it any time your requirements change. If you find that your program needs to use a new module or package, you use `pip install` to install the new module or package, and then immediately call `pip freeze` to create an updated requirements file which includes the new dependency.

There is one more thing to be aware of when installing and working with modules and packages: sometimes, you will need to have *different* versions of a module or package installed. For example, perhaps you want to run a particular program that requires version 1.6 of the Django package but you only have version 1.4 installed. If you update your copy of Django to version 1.6, you may break other programs that depend upon it.

To avoid this situation, you may find it useful to set up a **virtual environment** on your computer. A virtual environment is like a separate Python installation with its own set of installed modules and packages. You can create a separate virtual environment for each project that you work on so that each project can have its own set of dependencies without interfering with the requirements of other projects you might install on your computer.

When you want to use a particular virtual environment, you have to **activate** it. You can then use `pip install` to install the various packages you need into that environment, and run your program using the packages you have installed. When you want to finish working with that environment, you **deactivate** it. This lets you swap between virtual environments as necessary to work on your different projects.

Virtual environments are a very powerful tool for working on projects with different, and possibly incompatible, package requirements. You can find out more about virtual environments at `http://docs.python-guide.org/en/latest/dev/virtualenvs/`.

Summary

In this chapter, we learned about the various ways in which you can test your Python modules and packages. We learned about unit testing and how the `unittest` package in the Python Standard Library makes it easier to write and use unit tests for the modules and packages that you develop. We saw how unit tests use the `assert` statement (or the various `assertXXX()` methods if you are using the `unittest.TestCase` class) to raise an `AssertionError` if a particular condition has not been met. By writing various unit tests, you can ensure that your modules and packages are working the way you expect them to.

We then looked at the process of preparing a module or package for publication, and saw how GitHub provides an excellent repository for storing and managing the source code for your modules and packages.

After creating our own test package, we worked through the process of submitting this package to the Python Package Index. Finally, we learned how to use pip, the Python Package Manager, to install a package from PyPI into your system's `site-packages` directory, before looking at the ways in which a requirements file or a virtual environment can be used to help manage your program's dependencies.

In the final chapter of this book, we will see how modular programming acts more generally as the foundation for good programming techniques.

9
Modular Programming as a Foundation for Good Programming Technique

We have come a long way in this book. From learning how modules and packages work in Python, and how to use them to better organize your code, we have discovered many of the common practices used to apply modular patterns to solve a range of programming problems. We have seen how modular programming allows us to deal with changing requirements in a real-world system in the best possible way, and learned what makes a module or package a suitable candidate for reuse in new projects. We have seen many of the more advanced techniques for working with modules and packages in Python, as well as ways of avoiding the pitfalls that you may encounter along the way.

Finally, we looked at ways of testing your code, how to use a source code management system to keep track of the changes you make to your code over time, and how to submit your module or package to the Python Package Index (PyPI) so that others can find and use it.

Using what we have learned thus far, you will be able to competently apply modular techniques to your Python programming efforts, creating robust and well-written code that can be reused in a variety of programs. You can also share your code with others, both inside your organization and within the wider Python developer community.

In this final chapter, we will use a practical example to show how modules and packages do far more than just organize your code: they help to deal with the *process* of programming more effectively. We will see how modules are vital to the design and development of any large system, and demonstrate how the use of modular techniques to create robust, useful and well-written modules is an essential part of being a good programmer.

The process of programming

All too often as programmers, we focus on the technical details of a program. That is, we focus on the *product* rather than the *process* of programming. The difficulties of solving a particular programming problem are so great that we forget that the problem itself will change over time. No matter how much we try to avoid it, change is inevitable: changing markets, changing requirements, and changing technologies. As programmers, we need to be able to effectively cope with this change just as much as we need to be able to implement, test, and debug our code.

Back in *Chapter 4*, *Using Modules for Real-World Programming*, we looked at an example program that faced the challenge of changing requirements. We saw how a modular design allowed us to minimize the amount of code that had to be rewritten when the scope of the program increased well beyond what was first envisaged.

Now that we have learned more about modular programming and the related technologies that can help to make it more effective, let's work through this exercise again. This time, we'll choose a simple package for counting the number of occurrences of some event or object. For example, imagine that you need to keep a count of the number of animals of each type you see while walking across a farm. As you see each type of animal, you record its presence by passing it to the counter, and at the end, the counter will tell you how many animals of each type you have seen. For example:

```
>>> counter.reset()
>>> counter.add("sheep")
>>> counter.add("cow")
>>> counter.add("sheep")
>>> counter.add("rabbit")
>>> counter.add("cow")
>>> print(counter.totals())
[("cow", 2), ("rabbit", 1), ("sheep", 2)]
```

This is a simple package, but it gives us a good target for applying some of the more useful techniques we have learned in the previous chapters. In particular, we will make use of **docstrings** to document what each function in our package does, and we will write a series of **unit tests** to ensure that our package is working the way we expect it to.

Let's start by creating a directory to hold our new project, which we will call Counter. Create a directory named `counter` somewhere convenient, and then add a new file named `README.rst` to this directory. Since we expect to eventually upload this package to the Python Package Index, we will use reStructuredText format for our README file. Enter the following into this file:

```
About the ``counter`` package
-----------------------------

``counter`` is a package designed to make it easy to keep track of the
number of times some event or object occurs.  Using this package, you
**reset** the counter, **add** the various values to the counter, and
then retrieve the calculated **totals** to see how often each value
occurred.
```

Let's take a closer look at how this package might be used. Imagine that you wanted to keep a count of the number of cars of each color which were observed in a given timeframe. You would start by making the following call:

```
counter.reset()
```

Then when you identify a car of a given color, you would make the following call:

```
counter.add(color)
```

Finally, once the time period is over, you would obtain the various colors and how often they occurred in the following way:

```
for color,num_occurrences in counter.totals():
    print(color, num_occurrences)
```

The counter can then be reset to start counting another set of values.

Let's now implement this package. Inside our `counter` directory, create another directory named `counter` to hold our package's source code, and create a package initialization file (`__init__.py`) inside this innermost `counter` directory. We'll follow the pattern we used earlier and define our package's public functions in a module named `interface.py`, which we will then import into the `__init__.py` file to make the various functions available at the package level. To do this, edit the `__init__.py` file and enter the following into this file:

```
from .interface import *
```

Our next task is to implement the `interface` module. Create the `interface.py` file inside the `counter` package directory, and enter the following into this file:

```
def reset():
    pass

def add(value):
    pass

def totals():
    pass
```

These are just placeholders for our `counter` package's public functions; we'll implement these one at a time, starting with the `reset()` function.

Following the recommended practice of documenting each function using a docstring, let's start by describing what this function does. Edit the existing definition for your `reset()` function so that it looks like the following:

```
def reset():
    """ Reset our counter.

        This should be called before we start counting.
    """
    pass
```

Remember that a docstring is a triple-quoted string (a string that spans multiple lines) which is "attached" to a function. A docstring typically starts with a one line description of what the function does. If more information is required, this will be followed by a single blank line, followed by one or more lines describing the function in more detail. As you can see, our docstring consists of a one-line description and one additional line providing more information about our function.

We now need to implement this function. Since our counter package needs to keep track of the number of times each unique value has occurred, it makes sense to store this information in a dictionary mapping unique values to the number of occurrences. We can store this dictionary as a private global variable which is initialized by our `reset()` function. Knowing this, we can go ahead and implement the remainder of our `reset()` function:

```
def reset():
    """ Reset our counter.

        This should be called before we start counting.
    """
    global _counts
    _counts = {} # Maps value to number of occurrences.
```

With the private `_counts` global defined, we can now implement the `add()` function. This function records the occurrence of a given value, storing the results into the `_counts` dictionary. Replace your placeholder implementation of the `add()` function with the following code:

```
def add(value):
    """ Add the given value to our counter.
    """
    global _counts

    try:
        _counts[value] += 1
    except KeyError:
        _counts[value] = 1
```

There shouldn't be any surprises here. Our final function, `totals()`, returns the values which were added to the `_counts` dictionary, along with how often each value occurred. Here is the necessary code, which should replace your existing placeholder for the `totals()` function:

```
def totals():
    """ Return the number of times each value has occurred.

        We return a list of (value, num_occurrences) tuples, one
        for each unique value included in the count.
    """
    global _counts

    results = []
    for value in sorted(_counts.keys()):
        results.append((value, _counts[value]))
    return results
```

This completes our first implementation of the `counter` package. We'll try it out using the ad hoc testing techniques we learned about in the previous chapter: open a terminal or command-line window and use the `cd` command to set the current directory to the outermost `counter` directory. Then, type `python` to start the Python interactive interpreter, and try entering the following commands:

```
import counter
counter.reset()
counter.add(1)
counter.add(2)
counter.add(1)
print(counter.totals())
```

All going well, you should see the following output:

```
[(1, 2), (2, 1)]
```

This tells you that the value 1 occurred twice and the value 2 occurred once—which is exactly what your calls to the add() function indicated.

Now that our package appears to be working, let's create some unit tests so that we can test our package more systematically. Create a new file named tests.py in the outermost counter directory and enter the following code into this file:

```python
import unittest
import counter

class CounterTestCase(unittest.TestCase):
    """ Unit tests for the ``counter`` package.
    """
    def test_counter_totals(self):
        counter.reset()
        counter.add(1)
        counter.add(2)
        counter.add(3)
        counter.add(1)
        self.assertEqual(counter.totals(),
                         [(1, 2), (2, 1), (3, 1)])

    def test_counter_reset(self):
        counter.reset()
        counter.add(1)
        counter.reset()
        counter.add(2)
        self.assertEqual(counter.totals(), [(2, 1)])


if __name__ == "__main__":
    unittest.main()
```

As you can see, we have written two unit tests: one to check that the values we added are reflected in the counter's totals, and a second test to ensure that the reset() function is correctly resetting the counter, discarding any values that were added before reset() was called.

To run these tests, exit the Python interactive interpreter by pressing *Control + D*, and then type the following into the command line:

```
python tests.py
```

All going well, you should see the following output, indicating that both of your unit tests ran without any errors:

```
. .
---------------------------------------------------------------------
Ran 2 tests in 0.000s

OK
```

The inevitable changes

At this stage, we now have a properly working `counter` package with good documentation and unit tests. Imagine, however, that the requirements for your package now changes, causing major problems for your design: instead of keeping a simple count of the number of unique values, you now need to support *ranges* of values. For example, the user of your package might define ranges of values from 0 to 5, 5 to 10, and 10 to 15; values within each range are grouped together for the purposes of counting. The following illustration shows how this is done:

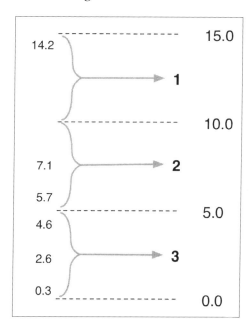

To allow your package to support ranges, you will need to change the interface to the `reset()` function to accept an optional list of range values. For example, to count values between 0 and 5, 5 and 10, and 10 and 15, the `reset()` function can be called with the following parameter:

```
counter.reset([0, 5, 10, 15])
```

If no parameter is passed to `counter.reset()`, then the entire package should continue to work as it does at present, recording unique values rather than ranges.

Let's implement this new feature. First off, edit the `reset()` function so that it looks like the following:

```
def reset(ranges=None):
    """ Reset our counter.

        If 'ranges' is supplied, the given list of values will be
        used as the start and end of each range of values.   In
        this case, the totals will be calculated based on a range
        of values rather than individual values.

        This should be called before we start counting.
    """
    global _ranges
    global _counts

    _ranges = ranges
    _counts = {} # If _ranges is None, maps value to number of
                 # occurrences.  Otherwise, maps (min_value,
                 # max_value) to number of occurrences.
```

The only difference here, other than changing the documentation, is that we now accept an optional `ranges` parameter and store this into the private `_ranges` global.

Let's now update the `add()` function to support ranges. Change your source code so that this function looks like the following:

```
def add(value):
    """ Add the given value to our counter.
    """
    global _ranges
    global _counts

    if _ranges == None:
        key = value
    else:
```

```
        for i in range(len(_ranges)-1):
            if value >= _ranges[i] and value < _ranges[i+1]:
                key = (_ranges[i], _ranges[i+1])
                break

    try:
        _counts[key] += 1
    except KeyError:
        _counts[key] = 1
```

There's no change to the interface for this function; the only difference is behind the scenes, where we now check to see whether we are calculating totals for the ranges of values, and if so, we set the key into the `_counts` dictionary to be a (`min_value`, `max_value`) tuple identifying the range. This code is a little messy, but it works, nicely hiding this complexity from the code using this function.

The final function we need to update is the `totals()` function. The behavior of this function will change if we are using ranges. Edit your copy of the interface module so that the `totals()` function looks like the following:

```
def totals():
    """ Return the number of times each value has occurred.

        If we are currently counting ranges of values, we return a
        list of  (min_value, max_value, num_occurrences) tuples,
        one for each range.  Otherwise, we return a list of
        (value, num_occurrences) tuples, one for each unique value
        included in the count.
    """
    global _ranges
    global _counts

    if _ranges != None:
        results = []
        for i in range(len(_ranges)-1):
            min_value = _ranges[i]
            max_value = _ranges[i+1]
            num_occurrences = _counts.get((min_value, max_value),
                                          0)
            results.append((min_value, max_value,
                            num_occurrences))
        return results
```

```
else:
    results = []
    for value in sorted(_counts.keys()):
        results.append((value, _counts[value]))
    return results
```

This code is a bit complicated, but we have updated our function's docstring to describe the new behavior. Let's now test our code; fire up the Python interpreter and try entering the following instructions:

```
import counter
counter.reset([0, 5, 10, 15])
counter.add(5.7)
counter.add(4.6)
counter.add(14.2)
counter.add(0.3)
counter.add(7.1)
counter.add(2.6)
print(counter.totals())
```

All going well, you should see the following output:

```
[(0, 5, 3), (5, 10, 2), (10, 15, 1)]
```

This corresponds to the three ranges you have defined, and shows that there are three values falling into the first range, two falling into the second range, and just one value falling into the third range.

Change management

At this stage, it seems that your updated package is a success. Just like the example we saw in *Chapter 6, Creating Reusable Modules*, we were able to use modular programming techniques to limit the number of changes that were needed to support a major new feature within our package. We have performed some tests, and the updated package seems to be working as it should.

However, we won't stop there. Since we added a major new feature to our package, we should add some unit tests to ensure that this feature is working as it should. Edit your tests.py script and add the following new test case to this module:

```
class RangeCounterTestCase(unittest.TestCase):
    """ Unit tests for the range-based features of the
        ``counter`` package.
    """
    def test_range_totals(self):
```

```
                counter.reset([0, 5, 10, 15])
                counter.add(3)
                counter.add(9)
                counter.add(4.5)
                counter.add(12)
                counter.add(19.1)
                counter.add(14.2)
                counter.add(8)
                self.assertEqual(counter.totals(),
                                [(0, 5, 2), (5, 10, 2), (10, 15, 2)])
```

This is very similar to the code we used for our ad hoc testing. After saving the updated `tests.py` script, run it. This should reveal something very interesting: your new package suddenly crashes:

```
ERROR: test_range_totals (__main__.RangeCounterTestCase)
----------------------------------------------------------------
Traceback (most recent call last):
  File "tests.py", line 35, in test_range_totals
    counter.add(19.1)
  File "/Users/erik/Project Support/Work/Packt/PythonModularProg/First
Draft/Chapter 9/code/counter-ranges/counter/interface.py", line 36, in
add
    _counts[key] += 1
UnboundLocalError: local variable 'key' referenced before assignment
```

Our `test_range_totals()` unit test is failing because our package crashes with an `UnboundLocalError` when we try to add the value `19.1` to our ranged counter. A moment's reflection will show what is wrong here: we have defined three ranges, `0-5`, `5-10`, and `10-15`, but we are now trying to add the value `19.1` to our counter. Since `19.1` is outside of the ranges we have set up, our package can't assign a range to this value, so our `add()` function is crashing.

It's easy enough to fix this problem; add the following highlighted lines to your `add()` function:

```
def add(value):
    """ Add the given value to our counter.
    """
    global _ranges
    global _counts

    if _ranges == None:
        key = value
    else:
```

```
        key = None
        for i in range(len(_ranges)-1):
            if value >= _ranges[i] and value < _ranges[i+1]:
                key = (_ranges[i], _ranges[i+1])
                break
        if key == None:
            raise RuntimeError("Value out of range: {}".format(value))

    try:
        _counts[key] += 1
    except KeyError:
        _counts[key] = 1
```

This causes our package to return a `RuntimeError` if the user attempts to add a value that falls outside of the ranges that we have set up.

Unfortunately, our unit test is still crashing, only now it fails with a `RuntimeError`. To fix this, remove the `counter.add(19.1)` line from the `test_range_totals()` unit test. We still want to test for this error condition, but we'll do so in a separate unit test. Add the following to the end of your `RangeCounterTestCase` class:

```
def test_out_of_range(self):
    counter.reset([0, 5, 10, 15])
    with self.assertRaises(RuntimeError):
        counter.add(19.1)
```

This unit test checks specifically for the error condition we found earlier, and ensures that the package is correctly returning a `RuntimeError` if the supplied value is outside of the requested ranges.

Notice that we now have four separate unit tests defined for our package. We are still testing the package to make sure it runs without ranges, as well as testing all our range-based code. Because we have implemented (and are starting to flesh out) a range of unit tests for our package, we can be confident that any changes we made to support ranges won't break any existing code that doesn't use the new range-based features.

As you can see, the modular programming techniques we have used help us minimize the changes required to our code, and the unit tests we have written help to ensure that the updated code continues to work as we expect it to. In this way, the use of modular programming techniques allow us to deal with changing requirements and the ongoing process of programming in the most effective way possible.

Dealing with complexity

There is no escaping the fact that computer programs are complicated. In fact, as the requirements for a package changes, this complexity only seems to increase over time—programs rarely become simpler as you go along. Modular programming techniques are an excellent way of dealing with this complexity. Through the application of modular techniques and technologies, you can:

- Use modules and packages to keep your code well organized no matter how complicated it becomes

- Use the standard patterns for modular design, including the divide-and-conquer technique, abstraction, and encapsulation, to keep this complexity to a minimum

- Apply unit testing techniques to ensure that your code continues to work as it should as you change and expand the scope of your module or package

- Write module- and function-level docstrings to clearly describe what each part of your code does so that you can keep track of everything as your program grows and changes.

To get a sense of just how vital these modular techniques and technologies are, just think for a moment how much of a mess you would end up with if you do not use them while developing a large, complex, and changing system. Without modular design techniques and the application of standard patterns such as divide-and-conquer, abstraction, and encapsulation, you would find yourself writing disorganized spaghetti code with many unexpected side-effects and with new features and changes spread throughout your source code. Without unit testing, you would have no way of ensuring that your code continues to work as it should as you make changes to it. Finally, the lack of embedded documentation would make it very hard to keep track of all the various pieces of your system, leading to bugs and poorly-thought-out changes as you continue to develop and expand your code.

For all these reasons, it is clear that modular programming techniques are vital to the design and development of any large system, because they help you to deal with complexity in the best way possible.

Being an effective programmer

Now that you have seen just how useful modular programming techniques are, you might wonder why anyone would not want to use them. Other than a lack of understanding, why would a programmer eschew modular principles and techniques?

The Python language has been designed from the ground up to support good modular programming techniques, and with the addition of excellent tools such as the Python Standard Library, unit tests, and docstrings, it encourages you to apply these techniques to your everyday programming practice. Similarly, the use of indentation to define the structure of your code automatically encourages you to write well-formatted source code where the indentation of your code reflects the logical organization of your program. These are not random choices: Python encourages good programming practices every step of the way.

Of course, just like you can write poorly structured and incomprehensible spaghetti code using Python, it is possible to avoid using modular techniques and practices while developing your programs. But why would you want to?

Programmers sometimes take shortcuts when writing programs that they consider to be "throwaway" code. For example, perhaps you're writing a tiny program that you expect to only use once, and then never need to use again. Why take the extra time to apply the recommended modular programming practices to this throwaway program?

The thing is, throwaway code has a funny habit of becoming permanent and growing into something much larger. Often, what begins as throwaway code becomes the basis for a large and complex system. Code you wrote six months ago can be found and reused in a new program. In the end, you never know what is throwaway code and what isn't.

For these reasons, it is a good idea to *always* apply modular programming practices to your code, no matter how large or small it might be. While you won't want to spend a lot of time writing extensive docstrings and unit tests for a simple throwaway script, you can still apply basic modular techniques to help keep your code organized. Don't just save modular programming techniques for your "big" projects.

Fortunately, the way Python has implemented modular programming makes it extremely easy to use, and after a while, you begin to *think* in modular terms before you even start writing a single line of code. I believe this is a good thing, because modular programming techniques are an essential part of being a good programmer, and you should practice these techniques whenever you sit down to program.

Summary

In this chapter, and indeed in this entire book, we have looked at how the application of modular programming techniques help you deal with the *process* of programming in the most effective way possible. Rather than avoiding change, you are able to manage it so that your code continues to work and is improved over time by the new requirements that are thrown at it.

We have looked at another example of a program that needed to be changed to meet an expanding set of requirements, and have seen how modular techniques, including the use of docstrings and unit tests, help to write robust and easy to understand code that improves as it continues to be developed and changed.

We have seen how the application of modular techniques is a vital part of dealing with the complexity of a program, and that this complexity only increases over time. We have learned that, because of this, the use of modular programming techniques is an essential part of what it means to be a good programmer. Finally, we have seen that modular techniques are something that can be used every time you sit down to program, even for simple throwaway scripts, and not something to be saved for your "big" projects.

I hope you have found this introduction to the world of modular programming useful, and are now starting to apply modular techniques and patterns to your own programming. I encourage you to continue to learn as much as you can about the various tools that surround good modular programming practice, such as the use of docstrings and the Sphinx library to auto-generate documentation for your packages, and the use of `virtualenv` to set up and use virtual environments to manage your program's package dependencies. The more you continue to use modular practices and techniques, the easier it will become — and the more effective you will be as a programmer. Happy coding!

Index

A

abstraction 104-107
ad-hoc testing 183
advanced module techniques
  global variables, dealing with 177, 178
  gotchas, importing 167
  imports, tweaking with sys.path 164-167
  local imports 163, 164
  modules and packages, using with Python
      interactive interpreter 173-176
  optional imports 161, 162
  package configuration 179, 180
  package data 181

B

backend 6

C

cache
  about 15
  using 20, 21
Charter
  about 70
  chart.py module, implementing 76
  code, refactoring 91-93
  designing 70-73
  generator.py module, implementing 77
  implementing 74, 75
  redesigning 89, 90
  requirements, changing 87, 88
  testing 87
circular dependencies 63

code, Charter
  PDF renderer modules,
      implementing 94-98
  refactoring 91-93
  testing 99, 100
complexity
  dealing with 221
continuous axis 72
coverage 187
coverage package
  reference 188

D

data storage module 25
dateutil package
  about 144
  reference 144
discrete axis 72
Distutils package
  submitting to 202
divide and conquer approach 104
docstrings 10, 211
dynamic imports 124-126

E

edge cases 187
effective programmer 221
encapsulation 107-113
examples, reusable modules
  about 143
  dateutil package 144
  lxml toolkit 145
  requests library 143, 144

Printed in Great Britain
by Amazon